Breaking Free
from our Cultural Obsessions!

Living Out Surprising Biblical Values in our Time

STEPHEN JONES

Order this book online at www.trafford.com
or email orders@trafford.com

Most Trafford titles are also available at major online book retailers.

Printed in the United States of America.

ISBN: 978-1-4907-4907-5 (sc)
ISBN: 978-1-4907-4909-9 (hc)
ISBN: 978-1-4907-4908-2 (e)

Library of Congress Control Number: 2014918317

Because of the dynamic nature of the Internet, any web addresses or links contained in
this book may have changed since publication and may no longer be valid. The views
expressed in this work are solely those of the author and do not necessarily reflect the
views of the publisher, and the publisher hereby disclaims any responsibility for them.

Any people depicted in stock imagery provided by Thinkstock are models,
and such images are being used for illustrative purposes only.
Certain stock imagery © Thinkstock.

Trafford rev. 10/17/2014

 www.trafford.com

North America & international
toll-free: 1 888 232 4444 (USA & Canada)
fax: 812 355 4082

Contents

Introduction vii

Chapter One 1
You Don't Have to be Efficient

Chapter Two 7
You Don't Have to be Consistent

Chapter Three 14
You Don't Have to be Successful

Chapter Four 22
You Don't Have to be Right

Chapter Five 29
You Don't Have to be Perfect

Chapter Six 35
You Don't Have to be Burdened

Chapter Seven 41
You Don't Have to Be Certain

Chapter Eight 48
OK, What Do You Have to Be?

Chapter Nine 55
Jesus, Liberator

Introduction

Are you culturally obsessed? Surely not! However, the truth is that all human beings are culturally conditioned. We are all the product of our society and its mores and values, its prejudices and assumptions. In his classic work, Christ and Culture, H. Richard Niebuhr states, "If Christians do not come to Christ with the language, the thought patterns, the moral disciplines of Judaism, they come with those of Rome; if not with those of Rome, then with those of Germany, England, Russia, America, India or China." (p.69, Harper and Row) We all look at reality through the prism of our own culture. While we naturally see reality from our own perspective, it is challenging to see reality through someone else's. If that is true for you, as it is for me, then we are culturally obsessed. We are so enmeshed in our own culture that it distorts our view of reality. Everyone is a cultural Christian - or at the very least struggles with it.

My mother tells the story of visiting her brother's church in Casper, Wyoming. And in a Sunday School class, a rancher in the church stated, "I can't understand the racial prejudice of you folks back in the Midwest." Yet, later in the same hour, he made a comment about the "drunken Indians" and their "worthless character." Through his cultural prism, he was sympathetic to African Americans who are an extreme minority in Casper. But he was prejudiced toward Native Americans who lived all around him. That is an example of how our cultural obsessions can distort our view of reality.

Often, as Christians, we dwell on moral laxity. We deplore our society at its worst. Gluttony, selfishness, violence, greed, materialism, immorality these are easily identified and condemned. And we assume that what our culture values at its best also describes the gospel of Jesus Christ at its best. In other words, to be a very good American is the same thing as being a very good Christian. Is there no difference?

What we will be exploring in these pages are some of the most respected values of our culture and how they may not represent the values of Jesus. Thus, we may be in for some real surprises. For example, our society values consistency. It values efficiency. But are these values of Jesus? Or are they cultural obsessions? Must one be consistent to be a follower of Jesus? Are Christians necessarily efficient?

In some of these chapters I will admittedly be "over-stating the case," so that we can recognize our cultural obsessions. Truth can better be tempered once recognized.

In truth, we have made the Gospel of Jesus Christ, already a challenging faith, even more burdened with cultural expectations that have little to do with Jesus' message. We have become so preoccupied with cultural strictures as to be blinded to the true cost of discipleship to Jesus.

It is easy to look back upon Hebrew scripture and see how the Jews became culturally obsessed with the religious practices of their neighbors creeping into their own faith traditions. As they worshipped false idols, it is easy to see their mistakes. Ezekiel prophesied, "What is in your mind shall never happen—the thought, 'Let us be like the nations, like the tribes of other countries, and worship wood and stone.'" (20:32) Even Israel's demand to have a king like their neighbors, a demand displeasing to God, shows their cultural obsession.

In these chapters, we will focus upon Jesus because, even though he also was a product of his culture, he was not obsessed with it. Jesus was able to rise above it and to proclaim the reign of God in counter- cultural ways. Probably one of scripture's best examples of this was the day Jesus returned to his hometown of Nazareth after he had launched his public ministry. At first, his kinfolk and lifelong friends were very impressed with what he had to say. But then Jesus lifted up two examples of God showing loving kindness to Gentiles rather than Jews. Jesus had to have known the reaction he would receive because he was addressing their cultural blinder of ethnocentricity. (Lk 4:14-30) He was rejected because of their cultural obsessions.

This is probably why Jesus was killed. He went up against the widely accepted values of his day and in so doing urged his followers to break free from the demanding expectations of their culture and enter into a radical commitment to the reign of God. In the same way, may we break free ourselves from our culture's demands in order to follow Jesus more radically.

These chapters were originally presented in a sermon series in the summer of 2014 at the historic First Baptist Church of Kansas City, Missouri.

Stephen D. Jones
Kansas City, Missouri
September, 2014

Chapter One

You Don't Have to be Efficient

Texts: John 12:1-8 and Luke 9:12-17

When it comes to efficiency, America is the dream of the world. American workers are efficient and productive. We are the world's leader in productivity per person. American productivity has increased 400% since 1950. Other nations, like the Chinese, South Koreans and Japanese have tried to emulate us, and when they do, their economies prosper. Americans are, by and large, hardworking. 85.8% of all American men work more than 40 hours per week. Americans work 137 more hours per year than the Japanese, 260 more hours per year than the British, and 495 more hours than the French. 134 countries have laws setting the maximum number of hours in the work week - America does not. We are the only industrialized nation with no legally-mandated annual leave from work. In terms of the number of workers who enjoy paid vacations, we are hopelessly in last place among the industrialized nations. And when we work, we tend to work efficiently.

To be efficient is to be productive without being wasteful. Energy efficiency is the best way to combat the impact of global warming. We now own a hybrid car, and it was a joy to see the mileage on a recent trip as we drove to the East Coast hovering around 40 miles per gallon. A very efficient automobile!

We strive to be efficient people · making the best use of our time and resources. Efficient people are practical, get-it-done types. Efficient leaders are admired for their crispness in action and word, wasting neither time nor resources. They do what must be done in the quickest, most cost-effective manner. Efficient people are well-organized, getting a lot accomplished with the least amount of waste. The more efficient you are the more successful you tend to be.

When your annual work evaluation reads, "This is one of our most efficient workers," you can expect a raise in compensation because business loves efficiency. To be inefficient is to be wasteful and disorganized. It is to manage one's time and tasks poorly. It requires a lot to accomplish very little. "The American Way" is built upon a devotion to efficiency.

Maybe our challenge is that we tend to turn all of life into work, and all of our time into productive time. Howard Ikemoto once said, "When my daughter was about 7 years old, she asked me what I did at work. I told her that I worked at a college and that my job was to teach people how to draw. She stared at me incredulously and then said, 'You mean they forgot?'" (p. 4, *Alive Now*, Jan/Feb, 2003)

Eugene Kennedy said years ago, "The hills are alive, not with the sound of music, but with experts trying to make the world run better. Look up 'management consultants' and you will find a long list of them. Americans have always been big on efficiency, time-motion studies, better mouse traps, higher compression ratios in their engines,...these have been a part of our national psyche for a long time now. Search the internet and every year brings a new set of books and resources on improved methods of management. Go to conventions and you will find that what is proclaimed as new is also proclaimed as efficient." (p. 133, The Pain of Being Human, Eugene Kennedy, Thomas More Press, adapted)

As a pastor, I attend a lot of meetings, and I dislike inefficient meetings. Time is wasted, extraneous conversations go off-topic, and decisions get delayed or postponed. The truth is, I love to be efficient. I love it when someone compliments me by saying, "How did you get all that accomplished?"

Yet, there is no more inefficient time than when I prepare sermons. I've prepared very few sermons when the ideas fell efficiently into place. Those sermons tend to be weak because they reflect a lack of struggle. An easy sermon is typically a bad sermon. The sermons in which I sit with a blank stare at a biblical text, or kick myself for choosing such a ridiculous topic, or find myself deleting more than adding, those are the sermons destined to speak to people. They are created out of struggle, not ease.

Is there such a thing as being efficiently exhilarated? Is there such a thing as being efficiently imaginative? Or being efficiently in love? I suppose a person could be very efficient in a marriage. Time spent with one's spouse could be well-planned, highly structured. Couples could plan ahead for conversation, that's Thursday night, or recreation, that's next Saturday, or for romance. A person could be efficient as a friend, never wasting a moment, scheming carefully the time allotted together.

But I don't think you can be efficient with the imagination, efficient with creativity, efficient with generosity, efficient with forgiveness, efficient with romance, efficient with play, efficient with prayer, efficient with exhilaration, efficient with gratitude, efficient with grief. It could be, and often is, that time wasted with a friend turns out to be the most valuable time. Time flittered away with a spouse, the most satisfying.

Even in business, efficiency can stifle creativity. The largest corporations, those most structured for efficiency, tend to produce the fewest innovations. While smaller firms, more casual and less structured, produce the most creative innovations. It is likely more efficient to have one boss who makes all the decisions. You don't have to waste time reaching consensus or collaborating. But the Japanese have proven that their collaborative decision-making model in industry is in the long run more productive because workers feel a greater sense of loyalty and investment.

Eugene Kennedy again said, "As a matter of disquieting fact, the world seldom runs efficiently. That is why there is always a market for those who would try, in each succeeding generation, to teach the world the lessons of efficiency all over again... Anybody be he executive, politician or pope, who thinks that he will be able to eliminate all duplication and get everything on a smooth and businesslike basis for any period of time, is bound to be frustrated if he is not ready to settle for less. That is why the battle goes on, the experts at efficiency blazing new and direct trails to the goals they can define so easily, while the jungle gradually closes in again just a few steps behind them... Perhaps Robert Frost was right when he said, 'Nobody was ever meant to remember or invent what he did with every cent!'" (ibid, p. 133, 134, 135)

The reality is that there is much in our world that is beyond our control. It is only when we divide up human experience into manageable bits that we begin to control it. But these little chunks of reality are often not real at all. Thus, we seek to control what cannot be controlled: the forces of life, the experience of being human, the search for truth, the necessity of purpose or meaning, the nature of human hope, the surge of emotion. We try to efficiently manage our world, while recognizing in our saner moments how futile our efforts are.

We don't have to be efficient. Human efficiency might be what Christ is calling us to abandon, to stop our incessant need to use, order, produce, and plan. And calling us from the burden of efficiently managing our lives so that we can allow God to rightly order our ways.

Consider Judas' objection in the Bethany home when Mary poured the expensive oil from the alabaster jar onto Jesus' feet, filling the room with fragrance. Judas was efficiently correct in objecting. Why waste the bottle of expensive oil? Couldn't it be put to more productive use? Why not sell it to feed the hungry? I've heard this argument so often in the church: why repair the steeple or remodel the restrooms when people are hungry in our society? Judas made a good point: Jesus is setting aside social concern for the poor by his tolerance of this wasteful extravagance.

Most churches have to watch their dimes and quarters: they cannot afford to be wasteful. And yet here is what Jesus is saying to Judas, "Set aside the poor right now. Be extravagant with the expensive oil. Go on, be wildly worshipful! Pour it on my feet, even though it will do my feet no real good, and it's plainly an inefficient use of resources. Go ahead, empty the bottle. The poor you will have with you always!"

Judas, like any good church treasurer, was trying to introduce businesslike and orderly procedures into Jesus' movement. Mary, on the other hand, was ready to sit at Jesus' feet and accept his teachings for what they were, even when it called for an action that appeared to be wasteful.

Judas' Way was to say: "My plan will work. I know what's best. Let's deploy our resources in the most business-like manner." And Mary's Way was to say: "I am prepared to listen, to follow, to take risks, to step outside the box of conformity, no matter the cost."

Eugene Kennedy again said, "Maybe the Spirit can only touch us and change us when we drop the armor of efficiency and are able to let ourselves out with all the rough edges of life showing. And maybe we harden our hearts to the Spirit when we worship the cool, uncaring gods of hard-nosed efficiency." (ibid, p. 136)

The disciples made the same error. Once when they were at the far stretches of Lake Galilee, away from towns or cities, they felt responsible for the 5,000 hungry souls who came to hear Jesus. (Lk 9:12-17) The disciples had already huddled, and among themselves they likely said, "We've got a management problem here. These people are getting hungry. And poor Jesus, why, he's too wrapped up in his parables to notice the lateness of the hour. Let's be efficient and reasonable, and break up his story-hour while there's still time."

When the disciples pulled Jesus aside to express their concern, he said to them, "You're worried about the wrong things. You've focused upon the wrong issues. You want these folks to eat? Fine. Seat them in groups of 50." Now, think about that for a moment. It's a crazy solution to a hungry crowd. Can you imagine trying to seat 5,000 people in groups of 50? That's 100 groups!! And for what purpose? There's no food anywhere nearby!

The story wasn't really about the lad and his loaves and fishes. The miracle is almost beside the point. The point is what Jesus taught his disciples, "You're worried about the wrong things. We can meet physical hunger. Here, take these loaves and fishes and feed the people. Yet, the real problem is not that these people have come here hungry and wish to be fed, but that they have come here empty and want to be filled."

Jesus taught the same thing in the Sermon on the Mount: "Look at the birds of the air. They do not sow or reap or (efficiently) gather into barns; yet your heavenly Father feeds them. Are you not worthy much more than they?... So, do not worry or say, 'What are we to eat? What are we to drink? How are we to be clothed?' It is pagans who set their hearts on these things. Your heavenly Father knows you need them all. Set your hearts on his kingdom first...and all these other things will be given you as well." (Mt 6:26f)

Our need to fill our barns efficiently with harvest to see us through the winter months may make life too comfortable. We can be obsessive about efficiency, trying to achieve our own outcomes instead of relying on God's outcomes.

"What I have developed through the writing of my novels was a sense of plot, and beyond that, a sense that perhaps life itself has a plot— that the events of our lives, random and witless as they generally seem, have a shape and direction of their own, are seeking to show us something, lead us somewhere. We are always free as in a way the characters in a novel are also free—free to run away with the story, free to be what they want to be no matter how hard the author may try to make them something else - but in the midst of our freedom, we hear whispers from beyond time...sense something hiddenly at work in all our working whose plot can make us truly and everlastingly human... I choose to believe that, from beyond time, a saving mystery breaks into our time at odd and unforeseeable moments.... There is no chance thing through which God cannot speak—even the walk from the house to the garage that you have walked 10,000 times before, even the moments when you cannot believe there is a god who speaks at all anywhere. God speaks, I believe, and the words God speaks are incarnate in the flesh and blood of our selves and of our own footsore and sacred journeys." (p. 95, 96, 77, The Sacred Journey, Harper and Row)

The serendipity of God breaking into our lives may not imply a passion for wastefulness or inefficiency. To be devoted to wastefulness is surely far worse than a devotion to efficiency. Jesus was sometimes efficient, sometimes not wasteful at all, and sometimes able to get much accomplished with very little.

However, we would do well to remember that there are two ways to respond to Jesus:

There was Judas' way, convinced that he could efficiently manage and organize God's way. And there was Mary's way, who felt no need to be in control or to manage her life, but rather to let go and let God do something more wonderful through her.

Let us not be devoted to efficiency, but rather liberated to follow Jesus' way no matter where it leads.

Chapter Two

You Don't Have to be Consistent

Text: Luke 18:9-14

Can't everyone agree? Consistency is a good thing. Students, children, partners and friends are caught off guard when we say one thing and do another. There's nothing more disconcerting than to be with someone who is totally unpredictable. It is difficult to teach or mentor if we are not consistent in our guidance or example. Being consistent is a valuable and laudable human behavior.

Yet, Ralph Waldo Emerson once said, "A foolish consistency is the hobgoblin of little minds, adored by little statesmen and philosophers and divines. With consistency a great soul has simply nothing to do. He may as well concern himself with his shadow on the wall." (Self-Reliance)

Some may find it difficult to accept, but Jesus wasn't always consistent. He tended to be spontaneous as to make his life difficult to summarize or formulate. To one person he healed, he said, "Go back home and report all that God has done for you!" (Lk 8:39), yet to most of the others he "...ordered them not to tell anyone what happened." (Lk 8:56 and 9:21) He healed many people of unclean spirits, yet he once said that when an unclean spirit goes out of a person, it comes back with seven other wicked spirits "...so that the man ends up worse than before!" (Lk 11:24f.) Even if you are Jesus, you can't have it both ways: if on the one hand you call the Pharisees "blind guides," "hypocrites," "fools," can you on the other hand talk about loving your enemies?

At one time, Jesus protected the Temple from destruction by running out the money-changers (Lk 19:45f), yet in the next moment he prophesied the Temple's destruction (Lk 21:5f). Once he urged his disciples not to watch for signs of the end of time for no one can know this. At another point, he describes to the disciples the signs of the end of time (Lk 21:25f). In one unusual passage, Jesus tells his disciples, "If you have no sword, sell your cloak and buy one…" "Lord," they said, "there are two swords here now." And he said to them, "That is enough." (Lk 22:35) Yet, twelve verses later, one of the disciples pulled his sword to use against one who had come to arrest Jesus. And Jesus responded, "Put up your sword, for all who draw the sword will die by the sword." (Mt 26:53) Again, in his Beatitudes, Jesus said, "Blessed are you who are poor, for yours in the kingdom of God." (Lk 6:20) And in his statement of ministry, he said, "The Lord has anointed me to preach good news to the poor." (Lk 4:18) Yet when confronted with what was likely the most valuable gift given him, he rejects the idea to sell the fragrant oil and give the money to the poor saying, "The poor you have with you always."

Is this a criticism to point out Jesus' inconsistencies? The truth is, he responded to each situation creatively. In forcing Jesus to the test of consistency, we put two situations of a different kind up against each other. Jesus saw no need to make all things consistent, whether he left a parable unexplained and obviously misunderstood, or whether he unveiled to his disciples his true destiny.

Ernest Campbell has said, "Jesus didn't reduce the mysteries of life to problems and then proceed to offer solutions. He allowed the mysteries to stand—such mysteries as life and death and time and evil and suffering and joy. He didn't offer answers; he made responses." (Seeds Magazine) And John A.T. Robinson adds, the public marks of the Christian life "…are mostly marks of paradox—of losing one's soul to save it, of identity through identification, freedom through service, resurrection through crucifixion." (p. 31, The Difference in Being a Christian Today, Westminster)

The gospel is full of contradictions, such as those Paul described when he said that Christians are "…sorrowful, yet always rejoicing; poor, yet making many rich; having nothing, yet possessing everything." (2 Cor 6:8b-10) Carlyle Marney once wrote, "…had you not noticed how all the Gospel narratives feature a set of built-in surges? There is a series of careening lunges from left to right. There is a wild sequence of cascades - he's up - he's down. The Gospel is split by a mighty contradiction. It's as if we have two irreconcilables in the same bucket.

Confessed as Lord, he says immediately, using a different name for himself, that the Son of Man goes up to Jerusalem to die. 'Christ is Lord,' they say. He says, 'Tell nobody!' He feeds the five thousand, then takes a boat overnight to escape the kingdom they wish to thrust upon him...The Teacher dines with an aristocrat but talks to a harlot who had wandered by. Born to be king, he has the air of a peasant. To his coronation, he rides a donkey." (p. 72-73, The Carpenter's Son, Abingdon). The Gospel, Jesus' story, seems to be at ease with contradiction.

In insisting upon consistency, we may fail being faithful to God's Word. For even if we were once on God's path, God has now veered to the right or left, and we have plunged on straight-ahead, consistent, but wrong. If the Bible teaches anything, it is that the kingdom of God isn't predictable. It takes us by surprise. It emerges at the least predictable times and places. It isn't under our control at all.

Our God is not a God of only straight lines, but a God as well of circles and detours and abrupt change of direction. We talk disparagingly of "going in circles" and so have convinced ourselves that God only moves in straight, consistent lines...the kind of lines that we can plot out on a piece of paper: predictable, reassuring, just as we would expect and just as we would desire. We want a God who is easy to figure out - easy to contain in our thought categories. We want a God whom we can take for granted - to do what God has always done and always will do.

Yet, in sending Jesus into the world over 2,000 years ago, in one time and one place, doesn't this represent an about-face, a change of direction? Jesus entered human history as a great surprise!

Why did thousands of years go by on earth before Jesus was known or his words were heard? I don't know. Why did God's Word in Christ take 33 years to be expressed - the tenure of his life on earth? I don't know. Why did it take 50 days for the Holy Spirit to come upon the church after the resurrection? I don't know. Why did the church meander through history, nearly losing its identity, almost lost in a dark age, before God raised up a Martin Luther to introduce a correction? I don't know. Why has racism in America survived a bloody civil war, in which it was supposedly defeated, before God raised up a Martin Luther King Jr. to penetrate the nation's conscience? I don't know. Why was apartheid allowed to stand in South Africa before a faithful servant like Desmond Tutu and a spirited leader like Nelson Mandela could crush it down and allow something more beautiful to emerge? I don't know. Why was God's word in Christ revealed to the Jews, rather than the Osage people, or the Taiwanese, or the Kenyans? I don't know.

I don't understand God's actions and God's timing. If I was the divine power in this world, I'd be consistent. I'd be predictable so you would always know who I was and what I stood for and what I expected. I'd spell it out clearly and stick to it through thick and thin. I wouldn't introduce surprise. I wouldn't sneak up on anyone. I'd do away with mystery and contradictions and ironies. I'd lay out everything plain, straight-forward and predictable.

And as if a reason was needed, that is precisely why I could never fill God's place in this world! With my logic, I'd do it all wrong. My desire for consistency can easily breed rigidity and legalism. As Paul wrote to the Corinthians, "For the wisdom of this world is folly in God's sight." (I Cor. 3:19) God's creative action defies sameness, repetition, or prediction.

Jesus approached those who were confident of themselves and told this parable: "Two men went up to the Temple to pray, one a Pharisee and one a tax collector. The Pharisee stood up and prayed about himself, 'God, I thank you that I am not like other men - robbers, evildoers, adulterers - or even like this tax collector. I fast twice a week and give a tenth of all I get.'" (Lk 18:10-12)

Let us consider for a moment the consistency of this Pharisee. Pharisees were very good people and we must take care not to look at them through a tainted window. When Jesus criticized them, he was criticizing his own teachers. If there was any Pharisaic trademark it would have been consistency. You always knew where a Pharisee stood. Here was a man who fasts twice a week and tithes his income. This man acts the same on Monday as on Friday. He is predictably good. And yet Jesus continued his parable, "But the tax collector stood at a distance. He would not even look up to heaven, but beat his breast and said, 'God, have mercy on me a sinner.' I tell you that this man, rather than the other, went home justified before God. For everyone who exalts himself will be humbled and everyone who humbles himself will be exalted." (Lk 18:13-14)

Consider Jesus' parable of the prodigal son. It was the brother who was consistently faithful to his father, never straying to the left or the right. He was loyal every day, one day to the next, to his father's expectations. Yet it was the prodigal son for whom the feast was thrown because "...what was lost, now is found." (Lk 15:11-12) Regardless of how unpredictable the prodigal had been, what was important at that moment was his safe return home.

A consistent life has much to commend itself, and caring persons will try to be consistent in thought and action. That is often how we can identify someone with integrity. But we must take care because God doesn't always reward human consistency. If our ultimate commitment is to harmonize our own word and deed, then we may fail to heed God's word and deed.

When I was a young pastor, I emerged from the flu season one year with a lingering headache. I felt assured it would go away, but it did not. I was functioning with less energy and patience, and was always distracted by this lingering headache. After several months, I finally made an appointment with my doctor. When I told my doctor that I was sure this wasn't caused by stress, I could tell by his hesitant facial expression that he wasn't so sure. Finally, my doctor's reluctant diagnosis was offered: "It's likely stress." Stress?!? I was having a fairly good year and I didn't have any particular problems at home or at work. It couldn't be stress!

My doctor prescribed some medication. I took the medicine and presto, the headaches subsided. It was stress. I wondered, "Maybe I am in the wrong profession. Maybe my work is doing this to me - getting to me more than I am willing to admit."

It wasn't long before our annual family vacation with two other pastors and their families. When I brought up my story, the other two pastors admitted to a recent struggle with stress. One of the other pastors has had a disease for years that is at least exaggerated by stress. The other had experienced dizzy spells through the winter. And then there was me with my headaches. So much for not fitting into pastoral ministry: it seems I fit in entirely too well!

I came home determined to stop taking the medication and try a different approach. The 23rd Psalm came to me in that moment. Whenever I found myself in a stressful situation, I began repeating the 23rd Psalm over and over. Even when I couldn't recall all the parts to the prayer in their exact order or wording, I continued and the psalm soon became an answer to prayer. Maybe a dozen or more times a day, I would meditate upon the 23rd Psalm and repeat it. And soon, the signs of stress subsided, the headaches disappeared, and I felt comforted for the first time in months.

According to the American Academy of Family Physicians, 2/3 of all office visits to family doctors are related to stress. Stress is now known to be a major contributor to six of the leading causes of death in our country. Three of the best-selling drugs are an ulcer medication, a hypertension drug, and a tranquilizer. One leading doctor concludes, "Our mode of life itself, the way we live, is emerging as today's principal cause of illness." A major study concludes, "Stress, to put it bluntly, is bad for you. In fact, it can kill you... Stress causes deterioration in everything from your gums to your heart and can make you more susceptible to everything from the common cold to cancer." (Jan. 11, 2008, *Association for Psychological Science*)

Instead of being persons whose lives are marked by trusting acceptance of God's will, we are more typically marked by a frenzied desire to reshape the world in our image.

Faith is a basic orientation of life. It has to do with the direction our lives are facing. Conversion has to do with turning around, repenting, in order to face God anew.

The Greek word for turning around is *metanoia*: to change one's way of being. The New Testament took this little-used Greek word and gave it meaning unknown before: "Greek society never thought of a radical change in a person's life as a whole, or conversion or of turning around..." (Dictionary of NT Theology, p. 357, vol. 1)

Throughout the pages of the Bible, God turns people around, introducing *metanoia*, and people find themselves interrupted and suddenly moving in surprising directions. It's happened to me countless times: I took early retirement three years before I began my current pastorate! Who could have predicted that?!

Peter may be scripture's best example. He began as a rough fisherman, then a hasty disciple, a weakling at Jesus' trial, and a wavering church leader in conflict with Paul. Yet it was upon this Rock that Jesus built his church. If true for Peter, how could it be any different for us?

This is what God does: calls us to repent, to change directions, to turn around, to follow at right angles from before. Ours isn't the task of looking back over our shoulders to identify God's inconsistencies. Our role is to trust that beyond our comprehension there is an inexplicable divine harmony at the heart of God's call.

The truth is, we don't have to be consistent. In any given moment, our task is to watch for God, who sometimes comes at us from such surprising direction and speaks through such unpredictable voices.

This watching and waiting for God - and not for our own consistencies - is surely the liberating word that Jesus had in mind when he said, "For whoever exalts himself will be humbled, and whoever humbles himself will be exalted." (Mt. 23:12)

Chapter Three

You Don't Have to be Successful

Text: Luke 4:1-12

We know this story well. It is the sequence of the story that is less well known, and perhaps even troubling. Jesus, a young adult, left his family in Nazareth to go down to the Jordan River, there to be baptized by John the Baptist. And when Jesus came out of the water, John and the crowd were astonished. A voice from heaven said to Jesus, "You are my beloved, in whom I am well pleased." (Lk 3:22c) We assume the story rushes on to a victorious scene where Jesus launches his glittering career: his baptism a strong launch for the teaching, healing and preaching that would follow. Yet the sequence moves in quite an opposite direction, as Mark reports, "Immediately afterwards, the Spirit drove Jesus into the wilderness and there he remained for forty days, and was tempted by Satan." (Mark 1:12-13, Jerusalem)

Luke finds this order of Jesus' life to be so awkward that he arbitrarily inserts fifteen dulling verses citing Jesus' genealogy from Joseph back to Adam. Only after having separated the glory of Jesus' baptism from his wilderness experience does Luke feel comfortable returning to Mark's sequence. Yet the fact remains that Jesus' time with God is followed by his time with the Devil. One wanders back to Job in the Old Testament, recalling when God and Satan "struck a deal" in order to determine if a good person could withstand the Devil's attacks. Here again the Devil is on the attack as Jesus is in the wilderness.

It is obvious that this story re-enacts sacred history of the Jews in their exodus from Egypt as they wandered in the wilderness. A wilderness in biblical time meant a wild area scant of vegetation, water, food or population. Matthew explains to his Jewish audience that Jesus fasted, a common form of Jewish piety. Fasting was an accepted devotional practice of abstaining from food, the discipline of relying solely upon God for sustenance. Yet, in the midst of this spiritual devotion, Jesus had to reckon with the Devil.

The Devil tempted Jesus three times. The story is told in the barest detail. The conversations between Jesus and the Devil required much more dialogue than the text provides. A simplistic reading may make what was obviously a tempting ordeal into a too-easy victory.

The Devil recognized that Jesus had gone for days without food. In tempting Jesus to remedy his physical hunger, the Devil said, "Go for the material, man! Feed yourself, because no one else is going to take care of you if you don't do it yourself. Take care of Numero Uno! Come on, I can see that you are hungry. Eat, man! Perform yourself a little miracle - you know you can do it! And who would know - no one is out here but you and me. You gotta have bread, man!"

The Devil truly tempted Jesus. There would be no need to include this incident if the temptation wasn't real. No doubt Jesus thought to himself, "I am hungry. I haven't been looking out for myself as I should. I've been too wrapped up in this wilderness challenge. Just one piece of bread isn't going to hurt anything. I do need to build up my strength and I do need a little nest egg, a little security to get me through."

Yet, in sorting through this temptation, Jesus was eventually able to see its selfishness. This could have been the moment that Jesus developed the later teaching, "Do not store up treasures for yourselves on earth, where moths and woodworms destroy and thieves break into steal. But store up treasures for yourselves in heaven... For where your treasure is, there will your heart be also." (Mt 6:19-21)

And so Jesus responded to the Devil, quoting Deut. 8:3, "Man does not live by bread alone." He refused to give into his own hunger. The Devil's first temptation was materialism.

In the second temptation, the Devil said to Jesus, "Look, man, why stop with just yourself? You can have the whole world! You want power? You want glory? You want fame? Man, I can give you all that and more! I can give you power over all the kingdoms of the world. You won't need to lift a sword. No one gets hurt. Just follow me and it can all be yours."

Once again, the Devil knows his subject. Jesus was an extraordinarily gifted leader and he did possess unusual authority and power. The world could have been his. Rather than defeat on the cross, Jesus could have been the all-time success story of history: the one person who made it to the top.

Yet again, struggling with this temptation, Jesus was able to see its selfishness. Quoting Deut. 6:13, he responded to the Devil, "You must worship the Lord your God and serve him alone." The second temptation was one of self-glorification.

In the third temptation, The Devil said, "Look here, Jesus, I've taken you to the top of the Temple. We're on top of God's House, man. This is where God dwells and you can conquer it and seize it as your own. You can take God's place into your own hands! If you're the Son of God, see if you can take the old man's place! If you jump off the Temple, there's nothing stopping you! They'll follow you all the way. Go ahead, Jesus, Jump!"

Again, Jesus considered the Devil's offer. He's weaker now, anyway. But Jesus again came to his senses saying, "Do not put the Lord your God to the test!" (Deut. 6:16) The third temptation was to challenge the power and place of God.

Here we have three remarkable temptations:

To seek material gain;
To seek one's own self-glorification, and
To challenge God's power and place.

What we have, in ancient story, is a copy of our modern prescription for success: seek material gain; seek praise and recognition for your own achievement, and recognize no dependence beyond yourself. The overall message of these temptations is this: the demonic is in the desire to succeed. The rungs on the ladder of success, the attempt to make it to the top, are stepping stones in the Devil's garden. A modern translation of the Devil's temptations is simply, "You gotta be rich; you gotta be admired; you gotta depend upon no one but yourself."

In America, success has always meant becoming rich, acquiring status or fame. When you've pulled yourself up by your own bootstraps, you're the real model of success.

Dr. Tex Sample, a noted authority on the religion of the American people, said years ago that our national religion is a "gospel of winning," which is why we dislike the poor, because we regard them as losers. Churches that have packaged the gospel of winning are booming enterprises that attract many who believe in such a gospel. These churches stress success, positive thinking, the spiritual reward of upward mobility, confidence and a buoyant enthusiasm. Because they have packaged our cultural allegiance to winning, they attract large crowds and interpret their success as God's blessing. (Taken from a lecture in Cleveland, 1983). Today, we call this the Prosperity Gospel and it is successful all across America and the Southern Hemisphere. The rich are those blessed by God. The poor are those shunned by God. What a tragic reversal of Jesus' true message!

Few American youth escape the message: if you want to be somebody, you must be successful in school, in dating, in marriage, in your career, in your material success, and in establishing a lifestyle that is "more, bigger and better" than your parents. You must live in the right neighborhoods, belong to the right clubs, select the right schools for your children and pass on the American dream to them.

Three older boys were in a huge debate over which of their parents made the most money. The first boy said, "My father is a lawyer, and he can win one case in court and make $40,000." The second boy said, "That's nothing. My dad is a surgeon and he can perform one surgery and make $50,000. The third boy's mother was a pastor, and not to be outdone, he said, "That's nothing. My mom preaches one sermon and it takes six men to carry out all the money."

Jesus was tempted by that same formula for success, interpreted by the Devil in ways that fit the customs of that day. To this formula, Jesus said, "No, I would rather be a failure by the world's standards."

And, in many ways, Jesus was a failure. He was born in an era when one's lineage was of ultimate importance to one's destiny. Scripture says that he was born of the house and lineage of David, but that came from his father Joseph, who, in fact, wasn't his biological father. Not only that, but Jesus didn't grow up in the City of David - but rather out in the sticks, in Nazareth, the backwoods of Israel.

To escape violence, his family fled as refugees to Egypt. When he was dedicated in the Temple, "...his parents were too poor to bring the normal offering for purification. Instead of a lamb, they brought two pigeons to the Temple... Since Jewish rabbi's received no fees for their teaching, Jesus had no regular income during his public ministry." (p. 68, Ron Sider, Rich Christians in an Age of Hunger, Thomas Nelson)

His disciples could hardly have been called a "Who's Who" of the first century: rough fishermen, hated tax collectors, mostly uneducated and unrefined. Despite all his attempts, Jesus failed to communicate his destiny even to his closest disciples.

It wasn't his enemies who betrayed him. It was one of his own. He couldn't even command the obedience of his closest followers. Peter denied him three times and he was supposedly one of the strongest. And the crowds, they loved him when he was in a healing mood. They listened when he spoke with authority. They cheered him as he approached the capitol city. But they turned the moment the chips were down.

He wasn't as appreciated as we might think. Ten lepers were healed, yet only one came back to say thanks. He had as many enemies as friends, and as many doubted him as followed him. He couldn't even succeed among the Nazarenes, his hometown folk. The only time he showed himself there during his years of ministry, he so offended the Nazarenes that they nearly killed him.

Jesus would not have won a popularity contest. The scribes were worried about his increasing popularity, but it was never enough to secure him a place of strength or power. When challenged, he typically had to defend himself single-handedly. Had he ever stumbled at a trick question asked of him, there was no one else to step forward. As long as he was viewed as successful, he was popular. When he became viewed as a failure, they left him overnight.

In America, we are so committed to a gospel of prosperity, a gospel of winning, that we have tried to re-make Jesus into a celebrity of his day, a superstar. We think that wherever he went he was met by enthusiastic crowds, falling at his feet. Sometimes, we view his death as being so required by God as to not see it as a failure.

We refuse to see Jesus' brokenness. What we really refuse to see is that Jesus didn't strive to be successful by the standards of his day or our own. He chose to become weak rather than powerful, wounded rather than whole, humble rather than exalted. We refuse to see Isaiah's prophesy embodied in Jesus' life and death: "he was despised and rejected of men, a man of sorrows, and acquainted with grief... he was despised and we esteemed him not." (Isa 53:3)

The Broadway musical written more than 50 years ago, "For Heaven's Sake," has a song entitled, "Some Career," that seems to characterize his failure:

"He was a flop at thirty-three
His whole career was one of failure and loss
But the thing that's so distressful Is he could have been successful
But instead of climbing up - he climbed a cross!"
(book and lyrics by Helen Kromer, 1963, Williamson Music, Inc. NY)

There is no sign of failure greater than the cross. It is a symbol that he was ultimately misunderstood and rejected. He was received as a failure before the Sanhedrin, before Pilate and Herod. He was a mocked Messiah hanging between two common thieves. And he died a broken and humiliated man. It is no accident that many churches in America offer only the empty cross, not the crucifix - because we don't like to see Jesus in this light: broken, humiliated, and weak.

Only God could redeem the failure of the cross, and from such a tragic loss, bring a victory, from death draw forth life, from humiliation offer salvation.

I remember speaking once with a business executive in my congregation. He said, "The pressure of my work this year has been very intense. I sometimes think I can't take it. But I know I have to. They want me to produce a new program with an unreasonable deadline, or I lose my next promotion. It's as simple as that." We were sitting in his new half-million dollar home when he made this remark. He had a boat, a vacation lodge, every toy a person could imagine. And I said to him, "Bob, what difference would it make?" And he looked at me as if I were from outer space. How could I be so naïve? What difference would it make if he failed, if he didn't get the promotion, if his climb to success was over?

I pushed my point, "Look at you, Bob. This home, it's lovely. It's probably more than you ever dreamed of having. You've already got every material thing anyone would want. What else do you need?" Bob responded, "But my family would think less of me if I did not succeed."

"Really?," I responded. "Why don't you ask them? Would they really think less of you if you gave up a promotion to spend more time with them? Or if you gave up a promotion so your life, and theirs, would be less stressed?" Bob grew silent, and then he said, "I guess I'd think less of myself if I failed in my career. I wouldn't be doing all I know I can do. My colleagues at work - they'd be disappointed."

I know what Bob was doing to himself - for I have had the same temptations and fears. I remember the day that I went from serving a congregation of 700 to a congregation of 150 - in fact, I did that twice in my career, leaving a highly-regarded downtown church to serve a much smaller, less well-known congregation. And I remember worrying both times: what will others think? Will this be perceived as a failure? Will I be written off - my reputation tarnished?

There isn't anything wrong with success if it means the attainment of one's goals or just doing good work. Except in a very limited meaning, failure isn't a legitimate goal. But our work or achievement must never determine our worth as persons.

There is a great difference in saying, "I am worthy because others recognize my success." And saying, "I am worthy because God views me this way."

William Willimon once said, "The temptation to try and earn our way into God's favor is especially appealing to people of middle-class backgrounds. Most of us, from the time we were children, have been told by Depression-era parents that we must work for what we want and that we can get what we want in life only by dedication, education and persistence.... We get trapped on a perpetual treadmill of getting and earning and achieving until the day when, having worked ourselves to death, we discover too late that the most important things in life cannot be earned or achieved. They come as undeserved gifts." (p. 30, The Gospel for the Person Who Has Everything, Judson Press)

I remember a friend telling me of the time when he served a new congregation. Soon, there was a vote taken to integrate his white congregation with a growing Hispanic congregation, also worshipping in the same building. When the vote was taken, half of the members of his congregation walked out, never to return. He quoted the moderator as saying, "We have just lost many members. Only God knows whether we have lost any Christians." This church was not successful. It had just lost half its membership. But it was faithful to the Gospel of Love.

The problem with striving for success, or with the Gospel of Prosperity, is that we are attempting to build our own kingdom of power and self-glory. And that is precisely the choice that Jesus faced in his temptations with the Devil: "Seek your own gain, your own glory, your own place in the world." In seeking these things, we give into the Devil's temptations. In standing against them, we follow Jesus' example.

In truth, we don't have to be successful! The temptations of success were as great for Jesus as for us. As he prevailed, so must we.

Chapter Four

You Don't Have to be Right

Text: Luke 10:21, Mark 10:17-27

The young man was born into privilege and wealth. His parents owned an olive press and a grove of olive trees. It was property held by the family for generations. Olive oil was one of the most marketable exports in Palestine and families who owned the presses were remarkably wealthy. The wealthy belonged to a powerful inner circle of the religious hierarchy in Jerusalem. Since the political power was held by the Romans, religion was the power commodity of the Jews. Wealth was seen as a sign of God's favor. The young man's father was a member of the ruling Jewish Sanhedrin.

Yet, when the young man was 12 year old, his father died. Foreign merchants in the city quickly took advantage of the grieving family and they lost their olive press and much of their wealth. From a position of prominence, the family lost their status and the respect of others. From being blessed, now they were cursed. The eldest son was not given the privileges that otherwise would have been his. He became bitter and disillusioned and wandered off never to be seen again.

Our young man, the second eldest, vowed to save the family name and restore their wealth as well as the favor of God. Ten years of imaginative ambition and the young lad, now a young adult, accomplished what he had set out to do. Now, his family owned two olive presses and more fields of trees than before. The young man built this impressive estate through honesty and perseverance. He was greatly admired, and at an incredibly young age, he was promised his father's seat on the Sanhedrin.

Yet, the young man turned down the honor. Having gained financial security, he was troubled by a lack of spiritual security. For all his good efforts, he did not feel that he had done enough to please God. His wealth did not feel like a blessing but a burden he had to maintain for the sake of his family's well-being.

The troubled young man was preoccupied with the most debated faith question of his day: how to gain eternal life. The claim of eternal life was relatively new and his people were divided. Most of his teachers believed that all would be judged by God, and those who performed meritorious deeds would win eternal life and the rest would be confined to hell. Only the special few would have the spiritual conduct to gain eternal life.

One day, the young man met a popular rabbi on the streets of Jerusalem, and he asked the rabbi, "What must I do to gain eternal life?" The rabbi thought, and in his hesitation a crowd gathered. The crowds loved to hear the wisdom of a rabbi. Finally, the rabbi answered, "You gain eternal life by giving more of your great wealth to the poor, for this is the most meritorious act of all, the surest way of amassing riches in heaven, to sacrifice for the widows and orphans." The crowd was pleased with the rabbi's wisdom as he walked down the street with his disciples following him.

Yet the young man had heard this rabbinical advice so many times before. And it left him feeling empty. He had already given a great deal to the poor and he felt no closer to God.

One of his friends ridiculed his concern, "My friend," he said, "You've already given enough money to buy eternal life!" But the young man was sure eternal life had no price tag, and he thought the rabbi's advice was just about that: buying his way into God's favor by performing acts of charity. But what about peasants? How would they secure eternal life, he wondered.

He had kept all the commandments. He acquired his estate without lying, killing or cheating. He had done everything right: "By the book."

His thoughts were right; his theology was right; his motives were right; his morality was right. And still, all his money could not buy him satisfaction.

He had heard about a Galilean rabbi. "He's very untraditional," people would say of him. "His ideas are unorthodox, yet he speaks with unusual authority--unlike other rabbi's."

Weary of tired answers, the young man decided to seek out this unusual rabbi. He left his business behind and journeyed north to Galilee. From village to village, he asked where he could find this teacher named Jesus. Everyone had heard of him; few knew his whereabouts. After several days, he found Jesus near the Sea of Galilee. This rabbi seemed unpretentious, accessible, just a normal Galilean.

He watched from a distance the way Jesus cared for the sick, the poor, and the troubled. In his fine linens and entourage, he stood out among those listening to Jesus. After several days, he finally decided to approach Jesus. "Good Rabbi, what must I do to win eternal life?" He had blurted out his life-question without even introducing himself.

Jesus looked at this righteous man and said, "You know the commandments?" And the young man responded proudly, "Yes, I know them all and have faithfully kept them since I was a child." Jesus looked steadily at him, and loved him. And then he said, "There is one thing you lack. Go and sell all you have, and give it to the poor and then come and follow me."

Well, the young man hadn't expected this. His great wealth was the only respect his family had in the world, their only security. Jesus' advice would send them back to their troubled past. How could he do this to his widowed mother? To his younger siblings who looked up to him for the financial security he had restored to their family?

What is intriguing about Jesus' response is how closely it parallels traditional rabbinical advice. The change of only one word separates the teaching of Jesus. The traditional advice was: "Go and sell more and give to the poor." And Jesus said, "Go and sell all and give to the poor."

Jesus was certainly not implying that if the young man sold his estate and distributed his income to the poor that he could purchase eternal life. The amount in his savings accounts or storage barns wasn't the criteria.

The criteria is whether anything, including what's in your savings account, stands in front of your relationship with God. Jesus actually said something even more radical to first century ears: that if your father gets in the way, be rid of him (Mt 10:37; 8:21). Rid yourself of whatever blocks the view. Seek God first and all else will take care of itself.

So the rich young man left Jesus troubled, because the financial security he had worked so hard to achieve, blocked his view of God. Jesus once warned, "What gain is it for a person to win the whole world and lose his very soul?" (Mk 8:37)

Perhaps the real truth of the story of the rich young ruler lies in the difference between right belief and right faith. Right belief has to do with the content of one's creed, the accuracy of one's dogma, the systematic ordering of one's convictions. In this, the rich young man excelled.

Right faith, on the other hand, has to do with relationship: being related to God in a vital way. And in this, the rich young man was lacking.

John Macquarrie has said, "We know God only because God lets himself be known, and therefore our knowledge of God is not the mastering, objectifying knowledge of the natural sciences, but is a knowledge suffused with reverence and gratitude.... But while God is not a thing to be grasped as an object that appears in the world, we would be equally in error if we thought that we could lay hold of God within our own minds... To put it bluntly, it is idolatry to think that we have ever grasped God, that we have comprehended God either as an objective fact 'out there' or as an exalted idea 'in here.' In all such cases, we are trying to take God into our possession. God transcends anything we can grasp or contain, and when we think we have God, the truth is that God has slipped through our grasp and we are left clinging to some pitiable idol of our own making. We can never know God by seeking to grasp or manipulate, but only by letting God grasp us. We know God not by taking him into our possession, which is absurd, but by letting ourselves be possessed, by becoming open to God's infinite being which is within us and above us and around us." (p. 55, Paths in Spirituality, Harper and Row, adapted)

The Good News is that we don't have to be right. We can even be wrong. We can have a misinformed theology, a mistaken idea, a wrong action. Jesus once prayed, "I thank thee, God, for hiding these things from the learned and wise and revealing them to the simple." (Mt 11:25) The word for simple here means infant, and it implies those who receive God's love on simple trust, without needing to reshape it.

You don't have to be right.

When I was in seminary, the work of an English religious educator, Ronald Goldman, was receiving wide attention. He did research on religious education in the schools of England, revealing that biblical concepts are far too complex for children to "correctly understand." Therefore, they grow up with distorted notions and eventually discard Christianity.

Goldman's research never rang true with me. What difference does it make if a six-year-old girl believes, as Goldman reported, that the Bible was "...dictated by God and Jesus took it down on a typewriter..."! (p. 14-15, Readiness for Religion, Seabury)

One mother recently said, "We've been letting our six-year-old son go to sleep listening to the radio. I'm beginning to wonder if it's a good idea. Last night, he said his prayers and wound up with, "And God bless Mommy and Daddy and Sister. Amen... and FM!"

I would suggest that no child turns from the faith of their childhood because of wrong beliefs. As they grow in intellectual capacity, they can correct themselves. I suspect that more turn away from faith because they weren't allowed to make mistakes, and constantly experienced adults correcting them.

Our son went through a stage in which one day he announced that he was an atheist. We kept talking, and I told him about an agnostic, and he immediately said, "Yes, that's what I am. That's what I meant." I might wish for more, but a little healthy agnosticism never hurt anybody...a questioning attitude, never being entirely sure. I went through my own agnostic period. Yet, every time he experienced a scrape in life, or faced a crossroads, I have always said to both of my children, "I am praying for you." And I did. He once told me to never stop praying. Another time he said to me, "Dad, I think I'm going to need your prayers." And then, he called me once and asked, "Would you say one of your prayers for me?" This isn't a matter of right belief. It's a matter of relationship: How do I relate to God? How can we ever stop asking that question?

The loftiest of our thoughts and the purest of our deeds cannot reach the mystery of God. Indeed, it is unnecessary to reach God because God has already reached us. This is the good news of Jesus Christ, the genius of Christianity. Incredibly, God has reached us! In accepting this, we can deepen our understanding of God.

John Powell was a noted professor of theology at Loyola University.

He wrote, "Some 12 years ago, I stood watching my university students file into the classroom for our first session in the Theology of Faith. That was the first day I saw Tommy. I had never seen a boy with hair that long. I immediately filed Tommy under 'S' for strange.

"Tommy turned out to be 'atheist in residence' in my course. He constantly objected, smirked and whined about the possibility of God. When Tommy came up at the end of the course to turn in his final exam, he asked in a slightly cynical voice, 'Do you think I'll ever find God?'

"I responded emphatically, 'No.'

"'Oh,' he responded, 'I thought that was the product you were pushing.'

"I let him get five steps from the classroom door and then called out, 'Tommy, I don't think you'll ever find God, but hang on, my friend, because I'm absolutely certain God will find you.'"

Mindless faith gives rise to fanaticism, superstition, sentimentalism, and simplistic thinking. All of these responses by the rich young man would take him further away from Jesus. The rich young man leaves the pages of scripture with the task of theologizing in his hands. Jesus had not done the thinking for him. He never does. It won't be enough for the young man to sell his estate. That wasn't even the point. He must understand how his riches were blocking his faith.

One point in the story of the rich young ruler I nearly missed. The story is told in all three synoptic Gospels in nearly identical words. Yet, Mark's Gospel, the oldest, includes a phrase the other two omit. Mark says that Jesus looked at the righteous man, loved him, and said, "One thing you lack." Those three words, "Jesus loved him," are unique to Mark's Gospel. When Jesus looked at the young man, he loved him, and told him the truth.

When I served in Boulder, Colorado, it was an era when many fundamentalist students would come to mainline pastors in an attempt to convert us to their new-found faith. As a progressive young pastor, I was a favorite target. I would try to avoid these conversations, or rather arguments, because they proved nothing.

One particular day a young man came into my office carrying a best-selling book at the time about the second coming and the final judgment of God. He wanted to know if I believed in that book and knowing it to be of questionable scholarship, I said, "No, I likely don't." He kept pushing the issue so I finally laid down a challenge. I said, "The author of your book misquotes the Bible." In the heat of our debate, I challenged him to open the book to any page, locate any scriptural reference, and I would show him how the author had mis-used the Bible. I was more than a little nervous by my audacity. The young man eagerly opened the book and randomly pointed to one, two, three biblical references. We went to the Bible and examined the text. Not once, or twice, but all three times, I showed a defiant young man, then a shocked young man, and finally a disillusioned young man that the author had indeed mis-used the Bible. After frantic efforts, we could not find an appropriate use of the Bible. He staggered out of my office, never to be seen again.

Later that day, I proudly told this story to a friend and she said to me, "Now what did that prove? You took something away from the young man, but what did you offer in return? You only proved that you were right and he was wrong. It doesn't seem that you shared any concern for him." I knew her words were true. I had forgotten to love him.

God loves us and cares even when we are wrong, cares even when we follow our mistakes, even when we make errors in judgment, even when we draw the wrong conclusions, even in our hasty assumptions. It isn't whether we are right or wrong that opens us up to God's saving love when we are lost or to God's healing love when we are broken. Cannot Jesus, our Liberator, be the one who looks into our lives, loves us, and gently helps us face the truth?

You don't have to be right. But you do have to be in relationship with the God of Truth.

Chapter Five

You Don't Have to be Perfect

Matthew 5:48

"Be perfect, as God in Heaven is perfect." How would you react if someone said that to you: "As God is perfect, so am I?" How audacious! How arrogant! How hopelessly out of touch! And yet, here it is in black and white, a part of Jesus' famous Sermon on the Mount: Jesus expects us to be perfect. Who can possibly live up to that? Can anyone claim to be perfect? Anyone close to perfection?

Do you know people who are perfectionists? That would be people who set up absurd levels of expectations, mostly on themselves, while striving for perfection. And they will always fail because we are human beings not human perfections. Perfectionists live in denial or self-blame.

And it's likely true that nearly all of us try to present our very best selves, the best view of ourselves to others. There's yet another well-known television pastor who has just fallen into disgrace. When I served in Seattle, there was a pastor who built up his congregation into the largest mega-church in Puget Sound. And his trademark was biblical expository preaching which went on 45 minutes - and crowds flocked to hear him. But he was also known for his cult-like leadership style. And today he is barely hanging on after 75 allegations have been brought against him by former and current members of his congregation. During my years in Seattle, this pastor could do no wrong. But his humanity, or perhaps lack of it, finally caught up with him.

Are there perfect parents? Even the best parents have shortcomings. I've said in recent years, partly in jest, that if you haven't given your children adequate cause to spend years as a young adult on a couch with a good psychiatrist, you haven't done a good job! Often, as parents, we expect perfection from our children. Any failure, any lapse of judgment, any mis-step, and we react with utter intolerance. As if we haven't had failures or mis-steps or lapses of judgment ourselves.

One of the great differences between Jesus and other rabbis of his day was their inclination to do the minimum with exactness. Do precisely what the Law requires. Nothing more is asked of you. Never stray one step to the left or to the right. And Jesus seemed much more relaxed. One could summarize what he said with this admonishment: "Do the maximum in the way that works for you." The maximum doesn't have to be done in a prescribed way.

Perhaps the best example was Jesus allowing his disciples to pick and eat corn on the Sabbath, a clear violation of the "letter of the law" as enforced by the Pharisees. "Look, your disciples are doing what is not lawful on the Sabbath." (Mt 12:2) Do the minimum with precision. Jesus respected the Sabbath and he certainly didn't encourage his disciples to disregard it. If possible, obey the Sabbath. However, more important it is to heal the sick, the feed the hungry, to clothe the naked. And if you have to pick a few ears of corn in order to reach for the maximum, go ahead. (Mark 2:23f) The scribes and lawyers were horrified at such compromises. They said, "No work whatsoever shall be done on the Sabbath! No matter what kind of hardship it may cause or what kind of sacrifice it creates or what kind of opportunity is missed, keeping the Sabbath is paramount." Jesus turned this around by saying, "Human beings were not created for the Sabbath, but the Sabbath for humanity." (Mk2:27)

Yet, Jesus defined the goal of service to God in much more rigorous terms than other teachers. "You have heard that it was said of old, 'An eye for an eye and a tooth for a tooth,' (Ex. 21:24), but I say unto you, 'If anyone hits you on the right cheek, offer him the other as well.'" Or again, "You have heard it said of old, 'You must love your neighbor and hate your enemy.'" But I say unto you, "love your enemies, pray for those who persecute you. For if you love only those who love you, why is that so exceptional? Even the tax collectors do as much." (Mt 5:38-39, 43-46)

The key difference between Jesus and the other teachers is where you can afford to compromise. Jesus saw the Pharisees in binding allegiance to their interpretation of the Law. But in so doing they sacrificed mercy and sacrificed their humanity. Jesus warned, "Be careful not to parade your righteousness before others."

On the other hand, the Pharisees saw Jesus compromising the Law, and, in the process, revealing his humanity.

Two princes were watching a group of street urchins out the palace window having a snowball fight in the palace yard. The princes were miserable because they weren't allowed just to be normal boys. In a minute, they slipped out a back door of the palace to join the fight. One mis-thrown snowball went crashing into a palace window, which sent the captain of the guard running after the boys. He stood them all in a straight line, yelling at them for their misbehavior. He walked up to the first boy and growled, "What's your name, boy?"

The lad took a stately step forward and said, "I'm Edward, Duke of York."

The Sergeant responded, "Oh, Yeah?" To the second boy he asked, "And what's your name, boy?"

The second stepped forward and said, "I'm Charles, Duke of Wales."

Again the sergeant growled, "Oh, sure you are!" To the third boy he demanded, "And what's your name?"

The third boy looked up at the other two, wiped his nose on his sleeve and said, "I'm going to stand with my buddies, governor. I'm the Archbishop of Canterbury."

"Be perfect, as God in heaven is perfect." The word in Greek which we translate as "perfect" is *teleios*, which is derived from the word, *telos*, which means end or goal, that toward which someone is striving.

Teleios, then, can mean seeking wholeness; it can also mean being full grown or mature. *Teleios*, translated as perfection, would never mean to be without blemish or error, with no sense of wrong or sin. That's over our pay scale as human beings. However, that was more or less the claim of many Pharisees in Jesus' day: "I know all the commandments and I keep them faithfully." Do the minimum with precision.

Actually, in the Sermon on the Mount, we find the word, *teleios*, again, when Jesus said, "Do not imagine that I have come to abolish the Law, but to perfect it." (Mt 5:17) Here, the English translators use other words, "but to fulfill it, or to complete it." Therefore, in Jesus' Sermon on the Mount when he said, "Be perfect," he more likely meant to seek fulfillment or completion. "Rather than do the minimum precisely, set your sights on the loving intent of the Law and do the maximum."

Paul wrote something similar to the Philippians, "I am no longer striving for perfection by my own efforts, the perfection which comes from the Law, but I want only the perfection that comes through faith in Christ, and is from God and based on faith." (3:9, Jerusalem)

We can now see in his Sermon that Jesus was criticizing other religious leaders for being "perfectionistic." They were worrying about abiding by the minimum the Law required - with perfection. Jesus, on the other hand, was urging us to seek wholeness, seek completeness, seek maturity. God's People are not to seek narrow legalism or claim porcelain perfection. God's People are to seek maturity and fulfillment.

You don't have to be perfect! The strange-sounding good news is that Jesus expects us to be human. Don't pretend to be otherwise. With Jesus as Lord, we are free to claim our full humanity and our full completeness in Christ.

Frederick Buechner, in telling his life-story, shares part of his brokenness, that while still a lad, his father poked his head into his room one morning, said goodbye and then went downstairs to take his life.

From the burden of this loss, Buechner writes, "When it comes to putting broken lives back together—when it comes, in religious terms, to the saving of souls—the human best tends to be at odds with the holy best. To do for yourselves the best that you have it in you to do - to grit your teeth and clench your fists in order to survive the world at its harshest and worst - is, by that very act, to be unable to let something be done for you and in you that is more wonderful still. The trouble with steeling yourself against the harshness of reality is that the same steel that secures your life against being destroyed, secures your life also against being opened up and transformed by the holy power that life itself comes from. You can survive on your own. You can grow strong on your own. You can even prevail on your own. But you cannot become human on your own." (p. 46, The Sacred Journey, Harper and Row)

Surely we have all been grieving the suicide of comedian Robin Williams. To us, a person of such fame, such accomplishment, such comedic genius, such wealth, such success, it seems like he had a perfect, idyllic life. Sadly, it was far from true.

You don't have to be perfect! The good news of the gospel would escape you if you were without blemish or sin - or if you pretended to be. If Jesus himself was presented in the pages of the Gospels as being perfect, how could we relate to him? When the Bible speaks of Jesus' perfection, it speaks of his unifying desire to seek God's will for his life. When Jesus was 12, he disobeyed his parents. They told him to leave Jerusalem in the company of Galilean friends. His mother and father and younger siblings had left with this group, but Jesus stayed behind on his own. Is that perfect, when a 12-year-old disregards the instructions given him and leaves no clue that he is doing so? No, but Jesus was seeking *teleios*, disregarding Joseph's instructions in order to find wholeness in dialogue with the leading scholars of his day. Do you see the difference?

Luke reports, "The boy Jesus stayed behind in Jerusalem but his parents did not know it." (Lk 2:43) Oops. A failure to communicate: exactly what is expected of 12 year old boys. "We might give you some latitude - but you can't go off on your own and leave us in the dark." In fact, his parents searched for him "for three days" before finding him in the Temple "sitting among the teachers." Mary said to her son, "Child, why have you treated us like this? Your father and I have been searching for you in great anxiety." (Lk 2:48b) Oops.

When cell phones first came out, we decided to purchase one for our teenage son. And the rule was: whenever we call you, wherever you are, you take our call. If you don't, you'll spend the next week at home. I think our son didn't really believe us, because on one of the first nights with his new phone, we called, and he didn't answer. He said he was busy with his friends. And he spent the next unhappy week at home. After that, when we called, he always answered. Mary and Joseph didn't have the luxury of a cell phone but they expected their son to obey them and to be where they told him to be. Scripture says that was the last time Jesus did this: "He went home with them and was obedient to them." (Lk 2:51a)

Instead of obeying his parents, Jesus was seeking *teleios* with his Heavenly Parent. He said to his parents, "Did you not know that I must be in my Father's house?" (2:49) I was seeking completeness, yearning for my aim in life, stretching to do what God has called me to do, seeking to fulfill God's vocation.

Jesus wasn't fully "shaped" when he was born. He wasn't capable of having a theological discussion with his mother while wrapped in swaddling clothes lying in a manger. Like all human beings, he developed. As he journeyed along in life, he explored and he learned. This incident of Jesus in the Temple at 12 is a shaping example in his life. His baptism in the River Jordan was also a *kairos* moment for Jesus - maybe the first time he sensed the Spirit of God calling him out as God's Beloved. And his baptism was followed by his temptations in the wilderness, a "baptism by fire," in which he was purified, strengthened, and prepared for the launch of his ministry which quickly followed. These three stories are typical of the many shaping influences upon Jesus.

Despite Jesus standing in for God and for us on the cross, the most human person you will ever know is Jesus. He taught us what it means to be fully and wholly human. His message was and is: "With one desire in your heart, seek God's will. Seek God's wholeness." You don't have to be perfect. Be who God created you to be. Be who God calls you to be. Be fully human. And when you fail at that, God will forgive you.

In this message, "Be perfect, as God in Heaven is perfect," it means Seek Wholeness as God is whole. Seek what God created you to be. But you can't be, and don't have to be perfect.

Remember: Jesus died, not for saints, but for sinners. That's really good news for me - and I also suspect for you!

Chapter Six

You Don't Have to be Burdened

Text: 2 Corinthians 9:7; Luke 22:39-46

There are such things as Necessary Burdens. Parenting, at times, can be a burden. Going to work in the morning, at times, can be a burden. Daily chores, at times, can be a burden. We all have our crosses to carry. It's what Jesus said. And the cross that we each bear on behalf of our faith can be burdensome and heavy. Consider those who have actually died for their faith - the ultimate burden.

But there are such things as Unnecessary Burdens. For many of us in the church, our greatest burden is that of duty. As responsible people, we feel obliged to do certain things. From the moment we get out of bed in the morning until the end of the day we are often motivated by a highly-developed sense of duty. We live by obligation. Isn't that what Jesus wanted?

Obligations have a way of "piling up." Seldom do obligations get met, and then go away. They travel beside us. Someone is hurting, "I should be there at her side." "I promised the committee I'd follow up on this. I'm obligated." "I have to spend time with my family tonight." All of these things are stated as "should's." I should do this and I should do that. And "should's" and duty go hand in hand. And they can be very burdensome.

One woman was particularly burdened about flying in an airplane. A pastor took his seat beside her, he noticed that she was wearing a cross and it pleased him to sit beside a fellow believer. But as the plane taxied to the runway, the woman began feeling very anxious. As the plane began to climb in altitude, she became very tense, clutching the armrest.

Finally, the kindly pastor said to her, "There, there, you needn't be burdened by flying. Just remember that Jesus said, "I am with you always."

The woman snapped back, "That isn't what he said at all! He said, 'LOW, I am with you always!'"

Low or high, (!) Jesus came to proclaim good news, not burdened news. We don't have to be burdened! Burdens, like obligations, have a way of piling on top of us, and we become so weighed down we can hardly move. Our entire lives can be dominated by obligation, by duty, and consequently by guilt.

Paul wrote to the Corinthians, "Each one should give then, as he had decided, not with regret or out of a sense of duty; for God loves the cheerful giver." (2 Cor. 9:7) Paul is referring to the offering to be taken for the poor in the Jerusalem church. It is an offering that is extremely important to him. By taking a substantial offering, it allows Paul to build bridges with James and Peter in the Jerusalem church, from whom he was often alienated. It was a tangible expression of unity badly needed in the early church. You might think that Paul would "pull out all the stops" and play on the guilt of the Corinthians. Who cares if they give gladly - give generously! Yet, for Paul, the motivation behind the gift was as important as the gift itself.

He is essentially saying, "Don't give out of guilt or regret. Don't give to please me. Give as you have decided so that yours can be a cheerful gift of the heart."

So many of us are burdened by the motivation of guilt or duty:

"It's expected of you."

"You really should do this."

"They want me to do this, so I guess I'll have to."

"I think you ought to do this."

"I'm obliged to pull through."

"We wouldn't have asked you, but no one else will do it."

The motivation in each of these statements is external, not internal. It's what others expect of us that is the motivating factor. What will others think? What do others expect of me? What must I do to gain acceptance? And often the real motivation is guilt:

"I don't want to sit with grandma tonight. Someone has to, and everyone expects me to do it. I'd feel guilty if she were alone."

As Christians, we give the language of obligation and guilt a special twist: we assume that it's in the Bible. Jesus must have a long list of things we should be doing, actions we ought to be undertaking. And therefore, Christians should feel guilty or burdened. We feel guilty over the things God wants us to do, and burdened when we don't get them done.

So often the church motivates by guilt and obligation. "We haven't yet made our budget. I've given all I intended to give. But they are really pouring on the pressure so I feel obligated to give more." Not exactly a cheerful giver, is it? "Everyone in my family wants me to stop smoking, or stop drinking, or stop cursing. So, I guess I have to try." How successful do you think this person will be?

The good news is that we don't have to be burdened by obligation or guilt. The good news of Jesus liberates us from a duty-bound obligation to the Law or anything external to our lives.

It's my guess that many people stay away from the church because they already live burdened lives - and they assume that if they joined the church - their list of duties would just expand. Their guilt would deepen because the church is known for dispensing guilt.

Jesus seems to understand that guilt and burdens are not good for us. In Matthew's Gospel, he says, "Come unto me all you that are weary and carrying heavy burdens and I will give you rest." (Mt 11:28) And in the Sermon on the Mount he says, "By worrying and stressing, can any of you add a single hour to your span of life?" (Mt 6:27) Clearly, living a burdened life is not Jesus' way.

There is another motivation that is easy to understand. Rather than doing something because I ought to do it, now I do something because I want to do it.

*"One of the things I most look forward to every week is sitting
with grandma. She's such a wonderful, wise woman, and I
cherish my nights with her, just the two of us together.
I won't let anything get in the way of that."*

It's rather easy to do things because I want to do it. We all have things we want to do and it feels good when we can act out of our own desires.

And yet for many of us we look upon this motivation with suspicion: "If you really want to do it, should you be doing it?" And our theology supports this: "It's not what we want that's important." But the gospels don't really say that. Jesus looked in the Temple upon the widow giving her mite. It wasn't the high proportion of her gift that he noticed: it was the fact that she gave without recognition, of her own free will. She gave because it was her great joy to do so.

The father welcoming home the prodigal son didn't think about the implications for the older brother. He responded because it was his deep desire to celebrate his younger son's homecoming. He did it because he wanted to do it. The Good Samaritan didn't stop to help the man beaten up on the side of the road because he was obligated. Actually, it was the other Jews who passed by who were obligated. No one expected it of the Samaritan. He stopped because he had compassion and he wanted to be of help.

Isn't it obvious when we do the things we want to do? "I love the children of our church and it's my great joy to teach them every Sunday morning." Isn't that a different motivation than someone who says, "They couldn't find anyone else, so I'm left teaching the children?"

Don't you think the children would know the difference?

I actually heard that when I was a child. I was in a rather rowdy Sunday School class of boys and no one could control us. So, finally, the toughest man in the church was recruited and he came into the class on the first day and said, "I don't want to be here any more than you want to be here. But if you boys don't settle down, I'll thump you on the head so hard you won't soon forget it."

That didn't settle us down at all. But the next year, we graduated into Mrs. Weaver's Class. And Mrs. Weaver was quite elderly and not so stable on her feet and had been teaching that class of third grade boys for many years. Many people thought they should ask her to retire because they were sure that we would take advantage of her. In fact, our dads gathered outside the classroom on our first Sunday with Mrs. Weaver and they had designed a plan to rush in and save her from our mischievousness. Actually, from the first Sunday in her class, we were perfect angels. Why? Because nothing was more important to Mrs. Weaver than teaching her class of third grade boys and we were another group to love and she loved the mischievousness right out of us. We were putty in her grace-filled hands.

While the motivation of doing what I want is healthy and valid, it cannot stand alone. A person who does only what he or she wants to do is basically selfish. The first motivation, that of living by obligation is unhealthy. And the second motivation, is healthy, but it cannot stand alone. A third motivation is necessary:

> *"I really don't want to sit with grandma tonight. But*
> *because I love grandma and I want the very best for*
> *her, I need to sit with grandma tonight."*

This motivation is also internal. This motivation is based upon personal priorities, convictions and values. There are times when we need to do things that we don't necessary want to do. But these times don't have to be times of guilt or burden.

Paul reminds the Corinthians, "Each one should give as he has decided." The key to needing is in our decision-making.

There are things about pastoral ministry that I don't like to do. In general, I hate recruiting people to do things. I fear their rejection and seem, at times, to take it personally. I never want to recruit people to do things. Yet, there are times as a pastor when I need to place challenges before people. I do it because I need to do it - not because I am burdened to do it.

In Gethsemane, Jesus fervently prayed not to face the frightening death and suffering that awaited him. "If it be possible, let this cup pass from me," he prayed. And yet, after hours of struggle, with sweat falling from his forehead like drops of blood, Jesus discovered what was ultimately important to him. To fulfill what God was calling him to do, he needed to step up and face his own mortality. We might paraphrase what Jesus said, "Nevertheless, not what I want, but what I need to do to fulfill my calling - that's what matters."

Jesus liberates us from the daily burden of duty and obligation, living a life of "should's." His reluctance at first in Gethsemane gave way to intentionality, not regret. He didn't feel forced to the cross. He chose it. And he offers this good news to us as well.

Guilt, duty, obligation, burdens - these really are lousy motivations.

So, please, hear the good news of Jesus:

Respond to things because you want to do them - or because you need to do them. "You don't have to be burdened."

Chapter Seven

You Don't Have to Be Certain

Mark 9:14-27

Are you certain? Are you absolutely certain? What does it mean to be certain? When it comes to matters of faith, can you prove that you are right? Of course, you cannot. Faith asks a set of questions that scientific inquiry cannot answer. The old gospel hymn answers the question correctly: "You ask me how I know he lives: he lives within my heart." (*He Lives*, by Alfred H. Ackley, 1933)

You can't prove that someone is in love with you. You can't prove that today is worthwhile. You can't prove that you have a soul. You can't prove that life has meaning. You can't prove that there is a Loving God and Creator of the universe. You can't prove that your life is on the right course. You cannot prove that generosity is better than selfishness. You cannot prove that Jesus is the Son of God. And you can't prove that there is eternal life. In fact, most of the really important things in life, you cannot prove.

The longer I walk by faith, I have become more certain about some aspects of my faith. I simply won't get in an argument with someone about whether God exists. I have experienced God on countless occasions in very real ways. I have less doubt and more certainty today that a loving and purposeful God exists. And I don't need to get in an argument about it. Nor do I necessarily need others to approve of or agree with my experience of God.

I am convinced that there is an eternal dimension to our everyday life on earth. When we view things from an eternal perspective rather than an immediate perspective, it adds length, texture and color to our otherwise mundane lives. There is such a thing as *chronos* time, one day following another, and there is such a thing as *kairos* time, times of momentous meaning or opportunity. And if we're only counting Monday, Tuesday and Wednesday, and not counting those times when we have seen evidences of God's reign breaking in to our lives and our world, we are looking at a flat world rather than a multi-dimensional world.

One little boy was drawing intently in his class and the teacher walked by his desk and asked him, "Daniel, what are you drawing." Nonchalantly, he answered, "I'm drawing a picture of God." The teacher said, "But no one knows what God looks like!" Daniel looked up at his teacher and said, "Well, they will when I get through."

What does confidence mean? That I have no doubt, no questions, no skepticism? If that is the case, then my faith is in trouble because doubt is not the enemy of faith. Not at all. Doubt ultimately is the primary vehicle to strengthen and deepen our faith.

When Jesus came off the Mountain of Transfiguration with his closest circle of disciples, they encountered a crowd gathered around the remaining disciples. It was a tense situation with scribes and lawyers nearby.

"What are you arguing about?" Jesus asked. The father of a boy with epilepsy stepped forward and told Jesus, "I brought my son to you, but your disciples could not heal him." Jesus looked into the faces of the crowd. He saw his own disciples, defensive, embarrassed, divided. He saw the crowd, impatient, hostile, disbelieving. He saw the scribes and lawyers, ready to pounce, full of derision. And he saw the father, frantic, searching, desperate. Jesus said, "O disbelieving generation! How long shall I put up with you?" (Mk 9:19) He is referring to his impotent disciples, the impatient crowd, the discouraged father and the haughty scribes. "Bring the child to me," Jesus said.

Immediately, at the center of attention, the young boy was thrown into a frightful seizure, falling to the ground, rolling around and foaming at the mouth. The gasping crowd jumped back in fear of what they interpreted as an evil spirit within the boy. "How long has the child been like this?" Jesus asked. (9:21)

The father tried to intervene to protect his son from hurting himself, but there was little he could do. He responded with great sadness, "Since childhood, and it has nearly killed him. If you can do anything, take pity and help us!"

The man's sincerity was obvious. His great love for his troubled son, his patience with him, was fully apparent. But Jesus hears in the father's voice his skepticism. "*If* I can do anything?" Jesus asked him.

"All things are possible if we believe."

And the father responded, "I do believe; help my unbelief."

Jesus turned to the child and said, "You deaf and dumb spirit, I command you, come out of this child and never return!" The spirit shrieked within the lad, convulsed violently, and came out. The boy lay on the ground before them. Someone in the crowd said, "He's dead."

At that moment, Jesus leaned over, took the lad's hand, and lifted him until he stood calmly before his father. The crowd gasped in amazement, and the father was filled with thanksgiving, and Jesus and his disciples withdrew to a private place.

The other two accounts of this story in Matthew and Luke speak only of the father's faith, not his unbelief. Yet, there would be no reason for Mark to include this if it had not been integral to the original story and event.

This is the last time in scripture we hear of this father when he said, "I believe; help my unbelief." Kierkegaard once said that the believer is like a trapeze artist who must let go of one swinging bar in order to reach out across the emptiness as the next bar swings toward her.

In other words, uncertainty is every bit as important to faith as certainty. Do you recall how uncertain Moses was when God called him to lead his people out of bondage in Egypt? I'm not a leader, Moses said. I'm not a public speaker. I couldn't possibly lead my people. He was filled with self-doubt as to the role God was calling him to take. And what about the tentativeness of Jonah, who didn't want to preach to the Ninevites and hoped they wouldn't repent? What about the tentativeness of Peter walking on the water for the first time, looking down, and sinking? What about Thomas, who couldn't believe in the resurrection based on the testimony of others: he was filled with doubt until he could experience it? What about Ananias who didn't want to go to Saul, because he was persecuting Christians, but the Spirit insisted: take the risk, go to Saul, and lead him into the light?

Harvey Cox stated that he was in the presence of Cardinal Carlo Maria Martini in 1995, when he said, "The line between belief and unbelief runs through the middle of each one of us, including myself, a bishop of the church." (p. 17, The Future of Faith, Harvey Cox, HarperOne)

Joan Chittister writes, "Like most people, I was raised on absolutes and categories, on rules and certainties. I was told that my destiny was in my hands, if I worked hard, I would succeed. If I lived a good life, I would be rewarded. If I prayed hard enough, worked long enough, lived a regulated life enough, God would help me and guide me and work life in my favor. But the absolutes faded, the rules changed, even my image of God became bigger than the little, tribal, national, male idol who cares only for white North Americans..." Chittister continues, "All the givens have changed and the rules with them. Built-in obsolescence is the new given. Things are made to be discarded or upgraded or replaced. Everything in life is in flux. Everything in life is simply another step, not the final step, in the process of becoming something else." And she concludes this section by saying, clearly, "the world is pregnant with uncertainty." (pp. 8-9, Scarred by Struggle, Transformed by Hope, Wm. B Eerdmans)

We feel that uncertainty, don't we? With Isis on a tyrannical rampage in Syria and Iraq, with the U.S. conducting bombing missions in Iraq once again, with Israel and the Palestinians in Gaza once again in protracted struggle with no easy solution, with Ferguson on our minds when even white Americans are forced to admit that growing up black and male in our society comes too often with two strikes against you.

Change is happening all around us. The world is no longer simple, if it ever was. Many of us were not nurtured as children to participate in the diverse world that surrounds us today. Did you know that the Shawnee Mission School District in the Kansas suburbs has gone from 13.5% minority students a decade ago to over 30% today? Over 38% of that district's children qualify for free or reduced lunch. How about that for breaking up your stereotypes? Did you know that across America, in all of our public schools, that children of color now represent 48% of all students? Did you know that, according to the Census Bureau, 50.4% of all children under one year of age are minority in America?

We've had a black President now for six years - but many Americans simply cannot adjust, cannot accept that the leader of the free world is not a white male. Ferguson has raised issues and questions that many of us have never faced before. There was a major article last weekend in the Kansas City Star which focused upon Christian evangelicals and conservatives who find themselves alien in a foreign land, pushed aside by cultural changes they cannot accept. For a while, these folks were in the mainstream but culturally, today, they find themselves thoroughly sidelined.

Who doesn't turn on the TV and see disgusting, appalling language and themes? How could you possibly steer your children or grandchildren around violent video games, movies and TV shows and access on-line that bombard them with values that you cannot accept?

Change is all around us. The week that Robin Williams committed suicide, our son called us one night utterly distraught. He plays in a band with another young man who had received health news that threw him in a crisis and he killed himself that night. Many people simply do not know how to live in these times. And no one of us fully escapes the paradox of life today. Chittister says, most of us "are seeking equilibrium, homeostasis, stability. We want to arrive." (ibid, p. 20)

And yet Jesus was into change. What does it mean when Jesus' first public word was, "Repent"? Repent means to change, to turn things around. For all of us, repentance isn't a one-time event. It didn't just happen to you once a long time ago and now it's over. Jesus introduced metanoia - the opportunity to change our very way of being. Conversion, not just once, but over and over again, was his invitation. Keep turning toward God and God's reign. Our God is a Transforming God.

"Every moment of one's existence," Norman Mailer wrote, "one is growing into more or retreating into less. One is always living a little more or dying a little bit." ("Advertisements for Myself" by Norman Mailer)

At the very beginning of my pastoral career, I could not have imagined the changes that would come to the church over the next 45 years. It is almost as if I am not in the same profession because pastoral ministry has changed so much and so fast. Just in technology alone, many older pastors like myself find ourselves foreigners in a strange land. It becomes harder to understand the world in which we live and therefore harder to pronounce a word of good news.

First Baptist Church of Kansas City has a set of historical pictures of the huge Men's Bible Class and Women's Bible Class - the largest in the world - that were a part of our church in the 1920's. The Men's Class at one time topped 50,000. What has happened? Where have the people gone? Nearly every main-line church is asking the same questions, with only a precious few exceptions. And I don't have the answers.

The truth is that if you are living a safe and secure life, free from doubt, oblivious to questions, with no struggle, then you are very likely completely out of touch with reality.

The ability to ask questions is how you found faith in the first place. Who hasn't asked: "How can this be? Is that you, Lord? Are you real? Are you speaking to me? How can I know? What is the meaning of this? How can I re-build my life after this calamity? What's my life- purpose? Do you have one for me, Lord? Do you really forgive? Really?"

The truth is Jesus loved questions. He asked questions throughout his ministry. The Greek word, *erotao*, means "to ask a question" is used 49 times in the Gospels. Another Greek word, *eperotao*, meaning "to ask" appears 52 times. In Luke, Jesus asked 89 teaching questions; in Matthew, he asked 85 teaching questions; in Mark, 47.

Marie Livingston Roy wrote, "Jesus showed an unerring ability to ask the penetrating question. With a word, he exposed the pettiness of spirit that prevented persons from receiving the fullness of life he offered. Glimpsing truth face to face, they were stripped of pretense, selfconceit, hypocrisy... Regardless of their response, they had each encountered God in the questions of Jesus." (*Alive Now*, March/April, 1981)

If Jesus asked questions then, don't you think he still asks questions of us today? And don't you think his questions of us would expose our pettiness of spirit, stripping us of pretense and hypocrisy?

In truth, questions lead to further inquiry, reflection and growth. Our call as Christians is not to avoid asking questions but to follow the questions that "come to us," as they lead us to deeper water. Faith and doubt are not opposites. Faith and apathy - faith and un-caring - those are opposites. Faith and uncertainty are but two poles of one continuum, obvious in the tension in the father's admission: "I believe; help my unbelief."

Paul's emphasis was not to speak of salvation in the past tense, as something that happened to us a long time ago. He speaks of our need to "work out our salvation," of becoming saved, of "being transformed... from one degree of glory to another," which sadly is sometimes missing from the church's vocabulary (*Phil. 2:12; I Cor. 1:18; 2 Cor. 2:15-16; Romans 8:18-25; 2 Cor. 3:16-18*).

To be a person with vital faith, I must constantly walk the line between belief and unbelief. Paul states to the Ephesians, Let us become "mature people, reaching to the very height of Christ's full stature." (4:13) I am aware of my "half-stature" in Christ and it is that awareness that helps me reach toward Christ's fuller stature within me. In reality, we must join this father in scripture as we each plead, "Lord, I believe; help my unbelief."

Elie Wiesel, a holocaust survivor, once said, "One can be a good Jew, or a good Christian or Buddhist, with God or against God, but not without God. One may be against God for the sake of His Creation. I quarrel with him, fight with him, make up with him, but I am never without him." (interview in *Chronicle of Higher Education*) In these outbursts of creative tension, we find ourselves standing on holy ground, unexplored ground, ground we didn't even know existed.

God is surely not frightened of our questions or our doubts or our uncertainties! Look at the Psalmists, who constantly complained to God, wondered about God's absence, and then came to that place of soaring and poetic language about God's faithfulness. "This doesn't make sense," they would complain. "Even so, I believe!"

Many have been taken by the writing of a young woman named Sara Miles. She was raised an atheist and knew nothing about Christianity. One day she wandered into St. Gregory's Episcopal Church in San Francisco. Arriving late, they were serving the Eucharist. And watching this, on sheer impulse she decided to partake of the bread and the wine. Yet, she disliked all the creeds and the "mumbling liturgy." She left the first service only with questions, nothing more. But she felt drawn to return again and again. And receiving that holy meal, Jesus' supper, she was compelled to turn that inward-looking congregation outward and began a feeding ministry in which 250 homeless and hungry people crowded into that tiny sanctuary. It was on the altar of that church that hungry people were fed every Saturday. Little did she know that she was re-enacting the ancient story: that at the Lord's Table of the earlier Christians, the poor were fed and found acceptance and the love of Christ. Her unbelief, her questions, brought hope, renewal, real food and holy food to literally hundreds of needy but hidden people all around that church. And it transformed her new congregation. (*Take This Bread, a Radical Conversion* by Sara Miles, Random House)

And thus we come to this good news: The first five letters of the word, "question" is "quest." Questions lead to a quest - and God's Living Spirit is always in the quest - for it is a saving quest - a quest of hope - a quest of life!

Remember, "You don't have to be certain."

Chapter Eight

OK, What Do You Have to Be?

Galatians 2:19-20, 4:8-9

In the other chapters, we claimed:

You don't have to be efficient or consistent. You don't have to be successful or right.

And you don't have to be perfect or burdened or certain.

That rules out a lot of things our society expects of us - and that we typically think are expected of Christians. And there's a lot of liberation for us when we don't have to dedicate ourselves to those things I just mentioned: "You're off the hook!" That's freeing!

The truth of it is, all Christians are both culturally-conditioned and biblically-conditioned. And we are often blind to the difference. Our faith is expressed within human culture. But so is the Bible expressed in human culture. We can see this in Apostle Paul at times - how his faith was expressed within his culture - and how he was sometimes blinded by this. Take for example what he wrote to the Corinthians, "Does not nature itself teach you that for a man to wear long hair is degrading to him, but if a woman has long hair, it is her pride? For her hair is given to her for a covering." (I Cor. 11:14-15) I don't happen to think that nature teaches this at all. I think Paul's culture felt that short hair for men was good and long hair for women was good. But that has absolutely nothing to do with the requirements of our faith - it's Paul's faith expressed through cultural blinders. A man with long hair or a woman with short hair can make wonderful disciples of Jesus Christ in our day. It makes utterly no difference.

The entire New Testament has cultural blinders when it comes to human slavery. Is there anyone today who doesn't know in their heart of hearts that human slavery is fundamentally evil? There is no way to sugar-coat it or excuse it: slavery is wrong. No exceptions. And yet the New Testament never goes that far, because the culture of that day did not go that far. As far as the pages of the Bible go, masters are to be kind toward their slaves - but it never demands them to liberate their slaves.

Here's another example: many Protestants come from a culture that has abstained from the consumption of alcoholic beverage. At the Lord's Table in many of our churches, we still drink juice, not wine, a reflection of our cultural heritage. What about scripture? We know that first century Jews drank wine and that Jesus drank wine and that what Jesus offered to his disciples at the last supper was bread and wine. A preference today for juice is cultural, nothing more.

I'm not suggesting that culture is negative. Human culture is the carrier of social values, behaviors, and the collective patterns of a human community. It encompasses the "natural expression" of human beings toward one another in one community, one tribe, one nation.

But we must always see our cultural values and the values espoused by Jesus Christ in creative tension with each other. And as we recognize the difference, to take on the values of Christ rather than of culture. That is what is meant by the expression to be "in the world but not of the world." (John 17:14-16)

Christianity is an incarnational faith. It must be embodied in the ethos of a culture. Yet we are also capable of standing apart from our culture and discerning what makes the way of Jesus different. Throughout this book, I've used the word obsession - we can be culturally obsessed and thus believe that whatever our culture espouses as good - must be good.

Recently, I was standing in a long line at a bank in the inner city waiting for a teller. And the line wasn't moving. I'm not usually very pushy in such situations. But I kept looking over at the vice presidents and the branch manager who were oblivious to our long line and doing nothing to assist the one teller who was working. Finally, I walked over to the branch manager and I pointed out to him that there was only one teller line open and eight people waiting to be served. He went in the back and pulled someone off their lunch break and things started moving. Now, you need to know the racial dynamic. I was one of only two white men in the line and the branch manager was white. Everyone else was African American.

The African American woman in front of me turned and said, "Thanks for doing that. I would never have the nerve to do that, even though I just took a class at my church teaching us to be more assertive." We ended up having a fascinating conversation about race. The truth of it is that if the branch manager had been African American, it is very unlikely that I would have pushed him to take action. All these things are culturally conditioned.

The woman in the teller line ended our conversation by saying, "Someday, standing before the Lord, it won't matter whether we are black or white because God loves us all and will treat us all the same. I can't wait for that day," she said. And I said, "Me, too."

When we lived for three months in the Philippines, we didn't realize that a Filipino would rarely deliver negative news to a foreigner. So, if you asked any question, and the answer was really "no," the answer always was expressed as a "yes." The only way you could tell their honest response was to wait and see how they acted. "Could we go to the market together on Tuesday?" The answer was always "yes," because they didn't feel free saying "no" to a foreigner. So, you just had to wait until Tuesday and if they didn't show up, the answer was no. If they did, the answer was yes. That seemed strange to us, but that's their culture.

One time when we were staying overnight in a Salvadoran farming collective, we all awoke in the morning, had breakfast, and all the men and younger women of the village were to go off and work in the fields together. And they just kept hanging around, sickles in hand, ready to go - but no one was moving. And I recall thinking, "Are these people lazy? Why don't they just get going?" They waited about 45 minutes with no activity - and it was the cool period of the day. Finally, one last worker arrived, very tardy, and they all went to the fields together. In their culture, if someone overslept, they all waited. It was their way of enforcing the idea that no one works until everyone works. And no one had to chastise the tardy worker because he knew well that he had just cost his community an hour of work in the fields. But that was their cultural way of handling the situation - quite different from our own where we likely would have fired such an employee, or given him a warning. No harsh words of any kind were spoken by the Salvadorans that morning.

In 1820, Isaac McCoy, an early missionary in Indiana and Michigan with Native Americans, baptized a Delaware Indian woman who was later criticized for wearing tribal ornaments in her ears. The woman replied, "My religion is not in my ears. My heart is no more affected by the jewels in my ears, than it is by any other part of my dress." Nevertheless, the woman said she would ask the missionaries and "if they say it is wrong, I will put them away." In response, McCoy wrote, "We never deemed it necessary to make innovations on the customs of the Indians merely for the sake of form or fashion. Their ornaments are esteemed a part of their dress. She was, therefore, told that the Great Spirit had not directed what should be the fashion of our dress. Different nations and different ages had their various modes of dressing, both in regard to comfort and comeliness. Religion consisted of a right disposition of the heart..." The Delaware woman kept her jewelry.

Thank you, Isaac!

It is natural to follow the demands of our culture. It doesn't require imagination as these demands are drilled into us from the day we were born. The statement, "You should be efficient." And the answer: "Everyone knows that." The utmost demands of culture are assumed to be beneficial. To question these cultural expectations is to act counter-cultural. Jesus was counter-cultural. Jesus' conflict with other religious leaders on how to keep the Sabbath is an example. The others were obsessed with keeping the Sabbath in one particular way with no exceptions. And Jesus, more relaxed, looked to the purpose of the Sabbath as a vehicle to serve God.

When we cannot recognize our allegiance to cultural demands, then we are easily obsessed with these demands. When we distance ourselves, then it is possible to follow the way of Jesus.

We are each called to make this affirmation: *"I am a culturally-conditioned Christian who tries to hold my values in tension with the values of Jesus."* If we try to live out every cultural value, no matter how beneficial, we cannot possibly have space in our lives for the values of Jesus.

Missiologist Leslie Newbigin stated over 30 years ago, an "...exciting and costly move is called for, namely a genuinely missionary encounter between a scriptural faith and modern culture. By this I mean an encounter which...holds up the modern world to the mirror of the Bible in order to understand how we, who are part of modern culture, are required to re-examine our assumption and re-order our thinking and acting." (p. 47. The Other Side of 1984, World Council of Churches, 1983)

Sometimes church leaders in the Third World say to us, "Thanks be to God you introduced us to Jesus Christ. But you brought him to us blind to the fact that your faith was culturally conditioned. Now we must take that biblical story, as you have done, and develop our own patterns of faithfulness in creative tension with our own culture. And it will not look the same." It is important for African Christians to be fully African as well as fully Christian. Or for Burmese to be fully Burmese while being fully Christian.

The question which I have yet to answer: Is there something that Jesus is calling us to be that transcends human culture? I think there is and I'd like to identify five things that come to my mind. True, no matter the culture.

First, if you are going to follow Jesus, be awake. Be alert. Be ready. Jesus repeated this over and over again, urging us not to be caught unaware, or to be caught asleep. But to be watchful. Be waiting. Be alert. And always, be ready, for when God's Spirit moves! (Mt. 25:1-13; Mk 13:32-37; Lk 12:35-40; Lk 21:29-36; Mt 24:44)

One little boy went to church with his grandparents. His grandmother sang in the choir and it really disturbed her when the grandfather would nod off to sleep every Sunday during the sermon. Finally, she decided to give her grandson fifty cents each Sunday to poke grandpa in the ribs whenever he fell asleep. The new plan worked great every Sunday until Easter. The church was packed, but grandma looked out and grandpa was sleeping and her grandson made no effort to wake him. After the service, the grandmother questioned the little boy, "Why didn't you wake up your grandfather? He was even snoring!

You knew I'd pay you 50 cents to keep him awake!"

The little guy responded, "Yes, Ma'am, but grandpa offered me a dollar to let him sleep."

Second, listen to God's voice speaking...through a flower, through a majestic mountain, through the relentless churning of the ocean's waves, through the rain, through a critic, through silence, through the innocent remark of a child, through a preacher, through the most secular person you know, through world events. Listen for God speaking - and be watchful for signs of God's presence...everyday! (Mt 6:6-7; 7:24; 10:14; 13:13-17; Mk 9:2-7)

Third, persevere. Jesus taught us not to give up easily, but to keep on keeping on. God rarely acts on our timelines but rather according to a much higher plan, usually hidden from us. So persevere. Don't give up and don't turn back. God is worth waiting for. (Lk 18:1-8; Mk 7:24-30; Mk 10:46-52)

Fourth, Repent. The first ministry words of Jesus were, "Repent, for the kingdom of God is at hand." Be willing to turn around, be willing to change course, be willing for God's transforming hand to come upon you. Don't just keep trudging along: repent. Give up your obsessions. Take an honest assessment of yourself. Change course. (Mt. 4:17; 11:20; Mk 1:14-15; Lk 13:5; Lk 19:1-10)

And finally, follow. Christianity doesn't ask that you chart your own course. Follow Christ's leading. Be a disciple, a follower. Your path will be different from mine, but, even so, follow Christ's leading. (Mt. 8:19-22; 9:9; 11:2-6; 16:24-26; Mk 1:16-20; Lk 6:46-49)

I'm sure other ideas could be offered, but that is at least a starting place.

What about you? Are you awake and alert? Are you ready? Are you listening and watching for God? Will you persevere? Will you repent and change course? Will you follow Christ in all ways? That's what we have to be and do.

Paul wrote to the Galatians, "Formerly, when you did not know God, you were enslaved to beings that by nature are not gods. Now that you have come to know God, or rather to be known by God, how can you turn back again to those powerless and bankrupt elements whose slaves you want to be all over again?" Eugene Peterson says, "How can you possibly subject yourselves again to those paper tigers?" (4:8-9) Peterson re-tells Galatians 2, "I tried keeping rules and working my head off to please God, and it didn't work. So I quit being a 'law man' so that I could be 'God's man.' Christ's life showed me how and enabled me to do it." (Gal. 2:19-20, The Message, The Bible in Contemporary Language, NavPress)

Let us not be obsessed with the demands of our culture. And let us not be blinded by those demands. We can waste a lot of time, energy and spiritual power by trying to be efficient, rather than be watchful for the in-breaking of God's reign. What are our "paper tigers?" Are they not to be found in obsessing over being consistent, obsessing over being strong, obsessing over being perfect, obsessing over being right, obsessing over being burdened, obsessing over being certain - when, in fact, none of these cultural expectations are "the real thing?"

Living up to the highest standards of our culture can be very demanding. It can require our all. And while we may be admired and respected by others, we might not necessarily reflect the values of Jesus. Let us break free from these cultural obsessions.

Chapter Nine

Jesus, Liberator

John 8:31-36

Many years ago, I was driving down Salem Avenue in Dayton, Ohio. Salem Avenue isn't just a street, it is, often, an urban experience and it was my route from home to my downtown church. The Avenue abounds with diversity, except early on Sunday morning when it is as serene as a rolling countryside...very "un-salem-ish."

On this particular Sunday morning, I was waiting at an interchange for the light to change. I have no explanation for what happened next. From out of nowhere, a man came into the street dancing with total abandon in front of my car. He was dressed in a traditional prisoner's uniform, handcuffed foot to foot with a chain about three foot long. His attire looked almost medieval, strangely out of place, even for Salem Avenue. Yet, here was this man, peering at me as if I was the one, all suited up with a tie bound around my neck, belted into my seat, locked into my car, and he, without restraint, in frolic and merriment, was dancing in God's wide outdoors with abandon. I was his captive audience.

My first thought was that this must be some kind of urban street theater troupe harmlessly entertaining antics for preachers and other folks out at this hour.

It was, however, no show. In a split second, my car was surrounded by police cars, sirens and a paddy wagon. The man half-heartedly tried to get away, but they quickly surrounded him, put him in the paddy wagon and whisked him away, all before the traffic light turned green! In an instant, now I sat in my car, alone, on an empty street, and more than a little stunned.

What a strange, graphic symbol of how we seek freedom in our society. The chained man acted as if he was free. There he was, dancing with glee on the street, ignoring society's rules about where pedestrians belong, oblivious to the fact that the police were seconds away. He was "in the moment" and enjoying himself. He thought freedom meant being care-free - and I was car-bound. He was unafraid of anything and I was, for a moment, a little alarmed as he peered at me through my window.

Of course, his chains told how free he really was. This self-deception is much less obvious when it comes to our lives. Often, we too are "dancing in the streets," oblivious to the chains around our lives, and those who would rush in and snatch away what little freedom we have.

The essence of what it means to be human, and what sets us apart from the rest of God's creation, is the freedom to decide what makes us fully alive. No other decision is so uniquely human. We are free to shape our lives. And through spiritual power, we can even transcend our lives, live beyond the limitations around us. We were created, unlike the rest of the animal world, to experience discomfort inside our own skins. Everyone knows that feeling. My dog always appears comfortable inside his skin. I often don't. My dog isn't stretching for anything. But I am stretching, reaching for something beyond myself.

We human beings face a question: to what or to whom will we give our lives? If we live only for ourselves, our lives will become burdened by such a narrowing choice. We cannot reach fulfillment living only for ourselves. We must reach beyond ourselves, transcending ourselves, to find a Bigger Scheme, a Higher Power, through whom we can fit the pieces together. That is why, in nearly all cultures, in all ages, people turn to God.

We must place our ultimate trust in something or (S)someone. If we place our ultimate trust with ourselves, then we will surely be disappointed in ourselves. None of us are capable or deserving of "ultimacy." Most children first place their ultimate trust in their parents. But what happens when your parents let you down?

I began my book, *Faith Shaping*, with this paragraph:

"'Why did you have the accident, Daddy?' five-year-old Brian asked in childlike innocence. 'Wasn't it the truck's fault?' I had been driving through Tennessee on a family vacation and had failed to stop our car in time before crashing into the back of a slow-moving truck. For months following the accident and during an extended period of recuperation for our family, Brian couldn't understand how I could have caused such an accident. 'Brian, I made a mistake while I was driving,' I would answer. But no matter what I would say or how often I would repeat it, it was beyond my five-year-old's comprehension. He remembered the accident, actually in a rather matter-of-fact way. But what he found unacceptable was that his daddy could make such a mistake. It was a faith issue for Brian. If a parent could make a mistake like that, then parents aren't fully dependable nor can they be fully trusted." (p. 13, Faith Shaping, Judson Press)

Do you remember the first time you learned that your parents were fallible or limited? That they couldn't solve all your problems or heal all your hurts? And when we place our ultimate trust and confidence in a friend, a lover, what happens when they let you down or even reject you? And when we place our ultimate trust in our employer, what happens when our employer lays us off after 30 years of faithful service just so they don't have to pay our pension? We can place ultimate confidence in making money, but we can't take it with us and money usually involves an empty chase. We can place ultimate confidence in our glamour or sex appeal, but we all grow older and lose some of it.

Paul Tillich said, the person "who is not able to perceive something ultimate, something infinitely significant, is not a (human being)." Something ultimate, something that transcends our finite limitations.

Something there is in human beings that wants to break out of the limitations, seek the ultimate or the eternal, seek a Truth or a Purpose that transcends the daily grind. "God" is the name many give to this Transcendent Reality.

In ancient Greece, a person was free in so far as he belonged to a people. Freedom referred to a free citizen, as contrasted with a slave or foreigner. The free person could decide his own affairs within the city-state. For the Greeks, a person who belongs, is free.

Today, we are more likely to define freedom as the abandonment of ties to other things, other causes, other people. We think liberty comes not from being constrained by commitments or relationships. We presume that unattached persons are freer than connected persons. Freedom implies a rejection of things that "tie us down." Like the man in chains on Salem Avenue, freedom is being care-free.

I believe as human beings we are compelled to give our lives to something. We give ourselves to an addictive behavior, or to our children, or to a career, or through art or creative expression. In reality, we are a stretching, reaching species, and those who refuse to give themselves to anything that is Transcendent become withheld or controlled persons. They compromise for something less than their full humanity.

By design, I believe that we were made by God for God. We were created to give ourselves to God. We have a God-sized inner void which only something Transcendent and Eternal can rightfully fill.

Ernst Campbell said years ago, "We keep clutching our Social Security cards, our pension plans, our life insurance, our bankbooks, and our stocks. And we want to know why we are not freed. Roberta Flack once recorded a song with the title that ought make any preacher stand up. The title, 'Let Pharaoh Go!' What a switch! We thought the action at the Exodus had to do with God getting Pharaoh to let the Jews go. But that was nothing. It didn't require much from God. A few dirty tricks and a little magic, and they were sprung! But what a time God had out there in the wilderness. The Hebrews couldn't let Pharaoh go! Some of them said, 'There's not even a McDonald's out here.' Others grumbled, 'Can't even use our Visa cards.!'" (*A.D. Magazine*)

Letting go of our allegiances to lesser gods is the first step to true freedom. While every idol and lesser god captivates, the Living God offers freedom. That to which we give ourselves can either enslave or liberate us.

Martin Buber, the famous Jewish philosopher wrote, "In pure relation (with God)...you have felt simply free...as in no other time or place." (p. 82, I and Thou, Martino Fine Books) Jesus modeled authentic freedom. He was the most liberated person to walk on this earth. He found authentic freedom in following God's purpose and design for his life. And he offers that freedom to us. No longer limited by the reality that stood in front of his face, Jesus viewed life with a liberating eternal perspective. Life can be fairly bleak at times when we look only at "what is in front of our noses." It can be hopeful when we look at life from an eternal perspective. It might not look great right now, but we know that ultimately, everything will be in God's hands and everything will be alright. I can relax and enjoy the present more when I look at today through eternal eyes.

Jesus said, "If you are truly my disciples, you will know the truth and the truth will make you free." (Jn 8:32) I offer you freedom, he said, and "if the Son of God makes you free, you are free indeed." (Jn 8:36)

Let me tell you the story of two young couples. One we met in Singapore. When we visited this island-nation, we were struck as to how advanced it was. It seemed to be at least five years ahead of America in terms of technology, innovation and social development. The young couple who were our hosts were upwardly mobile. He had started a highly successful design company. They had no kitchen in their elegant apartment. All their meals, in their fast-paced lives, were catered or eaten out. They were an attractive couple, but they also seemed in bondage to their break-neck schedules, their advancing careers, and their unquestioned obedience to the civil authority in Singapore, which held the keys to their financial success and upper class lifestyle.

We met another couple in the Philippines. They also were college educated, urban, sophisticated and held positions of responsibility. They, however, lived in a tiny shack with a dirt floor and rarely could afford meat or fish in their diet. Yet, it was this couple that seemed freer, more astute as to how the alluring enticements of their society were really a form of bondage.

The Singaporean couple was church-going, moral and law-abiding, but their culture had placed so many burdens upon them and their upward mobility was dependent upon those burdens. We Americans also chase after burdens we place on ourselves from which Jesus offers authentic freedom. We have made it so complicated and burdensome to be a Christian: we have to be right, we have to be certain, we have to be consistent, we have to be efficient, we have to be perfect.

When, in reality, we have only to be faithful - for Jesus offers authentic liberation. And when Jesus set us free, we are free indeed!

The End

Other Books by Stephen D. Jones:

Faith Shaping, Youth and the Experience of Faith
Revised Edition, Judson Press
www.judsonpress.com

Rabbi Jesus, Learning from the Master Teacher
Smyth and Helwys Publishing Co
www.helwys.com

Peaceteacher, Jesus' Way of Shalom
Baptist Peace Fellowship of North America
www.bpfna.org
(free leaders guide available on the website)
(available in English, Spanish, & Burmese)

"Christianity is an incarnational faith. It must be embodied in the ethos of a culture. Yet, we are also capable of standing apart from our culture and discerning what makes the way of Jesus different."